Nuts for the Food Gardener

Published in the United States by Garden Way Publishing, Charlotte, Vermont 05445.

Second Printing, June 1975

International Standard Book Number: 0-88266-043-8 paperback
International Standard Book Number: 0-88266-044-6 casebound

Nuts for the Food Gardener

Growing Quick, Nutritious Crops Anywhere

by Louise Riotte

with illustrations by the Author

FOREWORD

L et's face it! We are in the midst of a population explosion, and in the years ahead not only may be eating less but enjoying it less. As farm land areas decrease and the demand for meat increases we must find the means of supplying more and more people with nutritionally acceptable foods. The world food supply will become steadily tighter over the coming years, as even here in the United States our population increases to 270 million by the year 2000.

But consider this: a given area of land will provide food for man or it will provide food for animals, which are later slaughtered for meat. Food converted directly into the tissues of the feeder animal (or human) also is used for reasons other than tissue maintenance and growth. This means that about 100 pounds of plant food will support about 10 pounds of human tissue. On the other hand the 100 pounds of plant food that will support about 10 pounds of *animal* tissue, as meat will support only *about one pound of human tissue*. To put it another way, land used for growing plant food will support 10 times as many people as land used for animal food. And as pasture land decreases, meat will necessarily become less and less available and higher and higher in price. The time to begin preparing for this crisis is *now*, and nuts can provide a big part of the solution.

Nuts of all types, whether grown on trees or vegetatively, can replace meat or be used as meat extenders without losing their nutritional values. And nuts are easy to use — even may be pulverized in a blender for easy digestibility or converted into "nut milks", or added to fruit juice along with honey to make a delightful drink. Nuts are good body-building foods, too, are excellent for children and adults alike.

Filberts and Chestnuts will bear in about the same length of time as it takes a bed of asparagus to start producing. And Peanuts will yield a crop the same season they're planted. Walnuts and Pecans take longer but will make large trees and give abundant harvests. If you plant a few nut trees now you will be well ahead of the game in the years to come.

CONTENTS

1

WHY NUTS ARE SO IMPORTANT

Nuts rank high first for their food value. They are so high in protein that they can largely supplant meat or be used as meat extenders. Walnuts, for instance, are a rich muscle and body-building food, high in vitamin C and containing vitamins A, B^1 and B^2. Almonds, containing vitamins B^1 and A, are one of the most nourishing foods, and one of the richest nuts. The Hickory is helpful in cases of low blood pressure, while Pecans contain vitamins A and B^2. But we hit the jackpot with Peanuts, which are excellent for growing children and adults alike, containing the pantothenic acid vitamins B^2 and B^1 as well as vitamin E in the oil.

Proteins are vital to the body for the building up and replacement of cells and tissues. And they also produce a certain amount of heat and energy. While the body can store fat and certain amounts of sugar, it has no facilities for storing protein. Large amounts, however, are not needed, and from five to seven ounces of the right proteins per day is adequate for the average person. You can add most of this to your food in the form of meat or nut "meats". Nuts are easily digested when eaten with bulkier foods such as vegetables, cereals and fruits and they also add taste appeal. Think of those Walnuts and Pecans as tiny "beefsteaks"!

Nut trees serve a dual purpose in the home setting by providing both shade and food. What's more many kinds will grow anywhere in the United States. And modern, grafted nut trees are so quick-bearing, that one no longer need wait a lifetime to enjoy their harvest. The Peanut, which really is a vegetable, produces the same season it is planted.

Nut trees add immense value to rural or suburban properties. Native trees, which you can start yourself from seed in time will provide timber stands which may be worth more than money in the bank. Natives also may be grafted to produce quicker-bearing varieties of nut crops.

Nut trees help, too, as do other trees, to filter dirt, provide oxygen and cool the environment. They are, in effect, outdoor air-conditioners. They soften both storms and noise when planted reasonably near one's home, giving both shade and privacy while providing nesting places for birds which keep harmful insect life in check.

I value nut trees not only for their crops of nuts but for their abundant yearly harvest of leaves, which are so rich in soil-building nutrients. Even the shells, after the nuts are removed, are useful in many ways to industry, while pulverized hulls of many species are valuable as compost for gardens.

The most popular nuts — those most widely used — are the Persian or English Walnut, Pecan, Almond, Cashew, Brazil nut, Peanut and Chestnut. But others, less well known yet valuable, include the delicious Shagbark Hickory, the Pinon, or Pine nuts of the Southwest, and others whose range is even more limited, the Macadamia and Pistachio.

"Nut" actually is the popular name for a type of plant seed or fruit which is characterized by growth in a shell of woody fiber. "Nut" may mean only the meat inside or it may also mean the shell, and it may refer to the seed of the fruit, as with the Almond. The nut even may be one of a large number of seeds lying inside a cone, like the Pine or Indian nut. Nuts are marketed whole, "in-shell" or as shelled nuts, kernels, or nut meats.

The kernels of almost all edible nuts are highly concentrated foods very rich in protein, and possibly this is why they are so often called nut *meats*, making up an important source of protein for persons who cannot eat meat — in many countries a large part of the regular diet. Bread is sometimes baked from a flour made from the Chestnut, just as southwestern Indians pound Pinon nuts into flour to make bread.

The versatile Peanut is valuable for so many reasons there is simply not room to enumerate all of them. The great Negro scientist, George Washington Carver produced seventy-five products from the Pecan and discovered over 300 different Peanut uses in the course of his experiments, which ranged from instant "coffee" to soap and ink.

A 30-page booklet of recipes and menu ideas, compiled by 7,000 Peanut growers of Oklahoma, includes main dishes, Peanuts combined with vegetables, soups, salads and fruit dressing, breads, sandwiches, cakes and frostings, pies, Peanut and Peanut butter cookies, candies, ice cream, puddings and sweet sauces.

Did you know that 200,000 *tons* of Peanut butter are consumed in the United States every year? The U.S. Department of Agriculture, in its analysis of 751 commonly-consumed foods, ranks Peanut butter very near the top in at least six nutritional categories: food energy, fats necessary to maintain body balance, protein, phosphorous, thiamine and niacin.

Although in South America Peanuts have been ground and mixed with honey or cocoa for centuries, as a North American food it apparently was invented in 1890 by a St. Louis physician seeking an easily-digested, high-protein food for his patients. People liked the new "health food" so well that by the early 1920's it had become a staple throughout the nation.

Because it is so high in nutritional qualities a single Peanut butter sandwich or several tablespoons of Peanut butter in a recipe will add important values to the daily diet. The butter is over 26% pure protein, a percentage higher than eggs, dairy products and many cuts of meat and fish, which are known as protein foods. Besides, it is much more economical, especially if you grow your own. And if you are thinking of Peanuts as possible to grow only in the South, cheer up, for I will tell you later about the upright Peanuts which will mature in Northern gardens as well.

Leaving Peanuts for the moment let's take a look at the Pecans, rapidly becoming one of America's most popular nuts. They, too, make valuable contributions to the diet; for like meat, they supply protein, fat and thiamin (one of the B vitamins). A cup of Pecan kernels furnishes 740 calories of food energy, and just twelve halves will furnish about 100 calories.

Walnuts make a particularly fine, as well as tasty, diet contribution, too. And Black Walnuts especially, have a very wide range where they can be grown — in fact, in almost half of the United States. In the cold regions where they will not produce well, their Butternut cousin can be counted on to give good crops. I have found, too, that nut trees like fruit trees often will grow and produce well in areas where they are not supposed to, sheltered locations, "mini climates" and other factors making this possible. Windbreaks help, too, in areas of high altitude and drying winds. Slotted fences will break wind better than a solid one. The fences, which also protect the trees from roaming cattle or goats, need not be fancy; use poles about five feet high of whatever wood is available.

Lawn trees usually are shallow-rooted, so that often it is difficult to have smooth grass near them — or even grow good grass — and these are the trees that are uprooted by high winds. But not the deep-rooted nut trees!

For years I thought English Walnuts were almost solely a product of California. It is true that of the yearly United States' 55,000 tons produced California accounts for about 50,000. But don't let that stop you. This highly-prized, delicious nut will grow in Oklahoma as well as in many states even farther north. But you must choose one of the Carpathian types which will live and bear in all but extremely cold states like Minnesota or the Dakotas.

You don't have to wait a lifetime, either, for these nut trees to bear. The Burgess strain of English Walnuts in particular is very rapid and a well-grown tree may bear in five to seven years. The trees grow very large nuts having very thin shells, a highly desirable factor which always should be considered when making a choice of type.

Planting nut trees, whether one or a hundred, can be very profitable. It always is easy to sell surplus nuts of good quality at prices that seem to increase every year. If friends and neighbors don't buy all you wish to sell, an ad in the local paper or a small roadside stand probably will get you more customers than you can care for. If you don't sell your surplus, nuts of all types make exceedingly welcome gifts, especially at Christmas. Since most are harvested in the fall of the year they are in fine flavor for the holidays, mature but still sweet and good.

I have two Pecan trees, one native and one grafted, as well as one tree each of the Black and Carpathian Walnuts. I often ship their nuts to friends in other sections of the country or to those who live in apartments and have no land on which to grow trees; I shell them first to avoid bulk in shipping. How to do this easily is discussed further on.

Nuts are among our cleanest foods, too. Like eggs they have their own protective packaging, but are less liable to breakage and spoilage, making the trip from tree to table or hulling bench safe and tidy.

Unlike fruits and vegetables nuts will keep well after harvesting for a reasonable length of time. Pecans, for instance, will store in a cool place for several months without becoming rancid. Shelled and placed in an air-tight container they may be refrigerated even longer, and nut meats packaged in moisture-vapor proof containers can be frozen and kept a year or longer. In fact, I have some in my freezer now that are several years old.

Insects sometimes do pose a problem with nut trees, and occasionally squirrels steal them, but they are one crop that few birds bother. It's true that bluejays and flocks of crows can be a nuisance at times, however, and in a later chapter we'll discuss this. But the songbirds like the several families of beautiful red cardinals nesting in my Pecans, help control the insect population.

Maybe it appears that your homesite is too small to accommodate a nut tree. Not necessarily. Even a fifty-foot lot can find room for at least one nut tree and often two or three. It is true that many nut trees eventually do grow to a great height — the Black Walnut 100 feet and the Pecan 60 or more. But remember there are Almonds, which if you choose a hardy strain will grow wherever peaches will thrive, make beautiful 15 to 25-foot lawn trees and in spring are covered with lovely pink blossoms.

For even the tiniest yard there is the Dwarf American Hazelnut (from Spring Hill Nurseries), an attractive, hardy, thick branched small tree that grows only 12 feet tall. It has the added advantage that its nuts are easy to pick and easy to shell out whole. This lovely tree also bears when very, very young.

Wild Hickory nuts often are praised for their outstanding flavor, and since they do grow wild here in southern Oklahoma I can heartily attest they are different and delectable. But you don't have to find a wild tree to enjoy them. You can grow Henry Field's Shellbark (Kingnut) Hickory. This is the grand old shagbark which reaches a height of about forty feet and bears nuts that are easily shelled and are well filled with plump nut meats. It is hardy in Zones 8 through 4 which means it will live and bear even in parts of northern Montana and southwestern North Dakota.

Hickory wood's strength, toughness, hardness and stiffness makes it the world's foremost wood for tool handles, especially for hammers, axes, hatchets, picks and sledges. At one time it was extremely popular for wheel spokes and other wagon parts. Hickory also is an excellent fuel wood that yields a high quality of charcoal, and often is used for smoking bacon and ham.

While most of us plant nut trees for the harvest of nuts, we should not overlook their value as shade trees, too. Often, as with the Almond and Hickory, they are beautiful in blossom. Walnuts, Pecans and many others are exceedingly attractive because they grow with upright, symmetrical trunks and well balanced, many branched limbs. Do not overlook, then, the fact that Pecans in particular, while they may not bear nuts in the far North because of the shorter growing season, still will make beautiful trees for home grounds. And who knows, there may come a year when you will be lucky and they will bear Pecans as well, particularly if you are careful to plant them in a sheltered location.

Nut trees valuable as windbreak and shelter-belt planting, will grow from seed easily and more quickly than most people realize, making them relatively inexpensive. Paper-shell Pecans will not come "true" from seed and must be grafted or budded if you would have larger nuts — but this is easily done.

Notice that I said "larger" nuts — not "better" nuts. It's a well kept secret, but most of us in the heart of Oklahoma Pecan country actually prefer the smaller natives. They vary, of course, and some of them are larger and thinner shelled than others, but they have an exceptionally fine flavor, high oil content and a sweetness that some larger, better-known named varieties lack.

I have two Pecan trees in my yard, one grafted and one native. Of the two I honestly prefer the native. And I can always count on getting a harvest from the heavier shelled native tree, for it will bear a full crop in many years when the grafted tree does not. For marketing purposes, however, the larger, showier Pecans will bring a better price, particularly outside the state, and well-chosen varieties often compare favorably with natives in taste.

The point I am making here is simply the fact that if you plant nuts of good quality from native trees and do not overtop your windbreak you will still get some mighty fine Pecans practically free. But whether you plant Pecans, Walnuts or some other type of nut tree, these are some of the finest things your homestead or backyard will ever grow.

Here is something else to think about. While one is not likely to cut down any trees grown for the harvest of nuts just to get the timber, there are times when trees must be cut for varied reasons. Sometimes in older groves they need to be thinned out to allow room for those that remain. Sometimes a place must be cleared for buildings. Several years ago this became necessary when we built a home on our small ranch. We saved and cured the wood of the Black Walnut trees and my husband used a portion of the lumber to build furniture.

Another windfall came when a friend's Pecan trees fell under the axe because of a highway project. Occurrences like this are something to watch for, since nut woods are so highly prized for furniture veneers. Even the smaller limbs of these beautiful woods can be used in making jewelry of wood — pendants, pins, earrings and bracelets. Even nut shells, particularly those of Black Walnuts, can be made into pretty ornaments.

2

WHAT GOES ON
IN THE GROUND

The deep roots of many nut trees, particularly the long taproots of the Pecans and Walnuts, are very efficient miners of minerals. By doing this they unlock from the soil deep in the earth a store of inorganic nutrients necessary to life.

These elements are mainly potassium, phosphorus, nitrogen and calcium, the trace minerals and several others. While most of us never think about what's going on underneath the ground, the 20-year research by Emanual Epstein, professor of plant nutrition of the University of California and plant physiologist of its Agricultural Experiment Station, reveals that such trees are particularly effective gatherers because of their deep growing habits and their root systems which branch out by extension "root hairs." Growing out at right angles to the root axis, they reach out ever farther as they deplete the soil in their immediate area, continuing even during the fall and early winter when the above ground portions of the tree have entered a period of dormancy.

Knowing this one realizes how necessary it is to feed nut trees well to maintain their health and vigor and good bearing. They

17

cannot ask for help, but they have their own way of informing us of their needs. Take note of their health and supply them well long before they become starved, stop bearing or even die.

It has been calculated that about five percent of a tree's weight is in minerals. Organic matter and rocks have an important relationship to growth, too. And the more organic matter your soil contains the more readily will ground rock particles become available to the growing tree. This is brought about because the decay of organic matter produces carbonic and other mild acids which dissolve the rock particles.

In their natural state in the forest, nut trees shed their leaves each year and the leaf mold builds up naturally. But we, in our desire for neat yards, often rob them of the nutrients contained in this natural mulch — and then we wonder why they do not grow well!

Always try to duplicate conditions that exist in the forest. The closer we can come, the healthier our trees will be. If possible every three or four years give them a layer of leaves up to twelve inches deep. In time this will weather down to an inch or two thick layer of rich, black soil, and then you need to renew the blanket of leaves.

This will work every time, because it gives your growing tree its own natural food. Besides providing the necessary aeration and soil moisture this mulching will make minerals available to the tree's root systems.

You will get faster top growth, possibly by as much as three to five feet a year, if you will follow such a program. And this, of course, is also likely to bring your tree into bearing sooner. To avoid splitting, which sometimes accompanies rapid growth, prune off any excess terminal or end growth. This minor problem is easily overcome.

To make sure your trees receive all the elements necessary, apply along with the leaves a mixture of balanced minerals and fertilizers. It's a good idea to work in equal quantities by weight of cottonseed meal or dried blood (bloodmeal), dolomitic limestone, phosphate rock or bone meal, and wood ashes, granite dust or greensand.

For small trees set in open soil these nutrients can be spread and tilled into the earth. Larger trees or those whose roots are covered with sod may be fertilized by punching 18-inch holes in the soil with a pipe or crowbar. Be careful to slant them in toward the trunk. Make your holes two to three feet apart and cover the entire area beneath the crown out to the dripline. Fill

Dig holes for fertilizer under the tree's drip line.

all the holes with seven or eight ounces of the fertilizer mix, capping the holes with peat moss or topsoil.

While trees may live and even grow tolerably well in poor soil, you will be well ahead if you have a soil test made before planting — and this is true whether you plan to plant just a few trees or a grove of several hundred.

A soil sample submitted for analysis, should weigh about one pound. Only a portion of the sample is tested, even though the pound submitted may represent up to forty acres of land in some cases. This means that a one pound sample of soil must represent about 80 million pounds of soil if the sample is taken from the top 6 to 7 inches. When I am taking a soil sample from an area where trees are to be planted I like to go considerably deeper than this, using a soil auger or probe rather than a spade or trowel.

Half-inch core from center of each ½-inch slice.

The soil probe is probably the best and easiest to use if the soil is not gravelly or rocky. Soil is easier to sample and handle when it is moist, and you may take a sample even when the soil is too wet for plowing or tilling. Clay soil that is too wet may dry into hard clods or lumps, which should be broken up before they dry out. Place your dry, pulverized soil in an empty fruit jar or other container, labeling it with your name, address and area from which it was taken. Sometimes your County Agent has facilities for soil testing. If not, he can tell you where to send it.

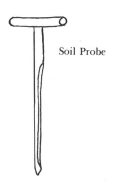

Soil Probe

When you fill out the soil test forms, be sure to tell the use you intend for the field or area. Whether you intend to plant nut trees or the shallower-rooted peanuts will make a difference in your soil's needs.

There are a number of different ways to obtain nut trees and some of them are "free." Seeds, of course, come under this heading, and we'll get into the specific "how-to's" later with individual species. For a quicker start you may wish to purchase trees that are offered by nurseries already grafted and available in several sizes. These may be bare root or balled.

Trowel

Of you may receive permission to dig up a small seedling tree and transplant it to your yard. Don't turn this down, because you can graft it later to a more desirable variety, but be sure to identify it correctly.

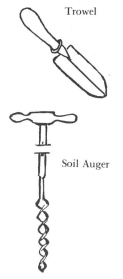

Soil Auger

I have given away dozens of the seedling Pecan trees which frequently spring up in my garden. They appear because we often mulch with Pecan leaves, and nuts are sometimes buried with the leaves when we turn these under. If I have a friend who asks for the trees I let them grow until fall, digging them when they are dormant. If no one wants them I pull the young trees out before the tap root has a chance to go deep.

If you do get permission to reclaim a small tree, it's good to know just how to dig and ball it properly, particularly if it must be transported some distance from your home. And freebies are fun!

HOW TO BALL A TREE

Start by clearing all weeds and loose soil from the surface, so you can create a smooth top for the ball. Next, mark a circle around the tree, before starting to dig, by tying a bit of soft string to the tree and affixing a nail to the other end to use as a marker. This done, dig around your mark with a sharp spade which will clip off excess roots as you go, but tie up the tree branches first to keep from breaking them as you work.

Of course the size of the ball will be determined by the size of the tree trunk and the type of tree. And the depth is determined by this as well. For even a small Pecan's deep taproot may require you to go down several feet. And if the tree is to live after transplanting you must get every bit of this. Remember, too, that when the tree is replanted the taproot (on all trees) must be buried absolutely vertical all the way down. Don't try to "cheat" on this or you will lose your tree.

Half of a burlap sack will serve as packing for the ball and should be wrapped around the upper portion of the tree as soon as possible. Pin the bag to the ball with slender nails.

After the top half of the ball is secured, keep digging until you have all the root possible to obtain. Place more burlap under the ball and pin this again with more nails. Then take another burlap bag and make an outside wrapping, pulling this as tightly as possible so there will be no air pockets. Now your tree is ready for transporting.

WHERE WILL YOU PLANT?

Practically all nut trees do best on deep, rich, well-drained land, but if your soil doesn't fit this description don't give up. Helped to a good start most nut trees are surprisingly adaptable,

Nursery Tree, 7-9-Foot Size.

and with the feeding program previously outlined you'll get good results.

A good start includes several things, and I cannot emphasize too much that the area where the trees are to be planted should be prepared well in advance of the day they are to be set out. Even the most carefully packed tree is subject to drying and it shouldn't remain out of the ground any longer than necessary.

Prepare a good sized hole for the tree, large enough to take the most developed root system. I like to go a bit further and break up the subsoil below, especially for Pecans or Walnuts — that long taproot again. Don't let this business of the taproot frustrate you though. Because a tree of this type, once it's established, can take a lot of punishment that plants with shallower roots cannot.

Nut trees even now are not expensive in comparison to their value. But if they fail to grow you will lose a year or two of time as well as the price of a new tree. So give them every chance by getting the planting site prepared well ahead of the time of purchase and shipment.

If the trees are to be spring planted you can give both yourself and the tree a break by preparing the planting site in the fall. Dig your hole for the size tree you plan to place in it and refill the hole with well-decomposed compost, or mix rotted manure with leaf mold and the soil you have removed. Cover the spot loosely with branches. This will allow moisture to enter but prevent the soil from packing. In the spring when your tree arrives, this loose "plug" of soil can be easily removed and the tree planted without delay.

By using this method the newly planted tree will develop a strong root system quickly making a rapid growth that will surprise and delight you. It may even come into bearing a year or so earlier than it would if the roots had to fight through tight, hard-packed soil. With such a head start you also may expect your tree to be stronger and more disease-resistant, for rapidly-growing plants are less subject to injury from insects and disease. Another plus you will probably note is that earthworms have arrived to feast on the organically rich soil. They will aerate the soil and enrich it further with their castings.

Nut trees will thrive under a broad range of soils and locations but, as with other plants, they do have a preference. Ideal conditions always produce better results. If you have a large acreage to choose from and plan to produce a commercial crop, selection of the right soil and location is important

Keep root system moist. Plant at once.

Trim the root system.

If not planted immediately, heel into moist soil.

Prune the top.

particularly.

Well-drained, loose subsoils are always best since practically all nut trees are very deep rooted, but there should be enough organic matter to retain sufficient moisture between rains. Swampy soils or those underlaid with solid rock are not suitable. Neither are dry windswept slopes, particularly if they are sandy or gravelly. Nor will nut trees tolerate extremes of either acid or alkaline soils, though their tolerance varies with individual species.

Almonds, Filberts and Hickories prefer neutral to slightly acid soils. Butternuts, Pecans, Black and English Walnuts range from slightly acid to slightly alkaline. The Chestnuts like moderate to slightly acid soil. As I noted before, a soil test will give you accurate information on the type of soil you have to work with.

When preparing to plant nut trees it is important to keep the roots moist at all times, protecting them from the sun and wind. Since a portion of the root system unavoidably is lost at the time of digging, this usually leaves more top than the remaining roots can properly support. Because of this, it is best to remove from a third to a half of the top at planting time, or even to cut the top back to about one foot. This seems severe, but the survival of your tree may depend on it. After the root becomes well established a new and better top will develop rapidly to take its place, and you will be well paid for doing this pruning.

Set your new tree (but not an Almond) slightly deeper than it grew in the nursery — you will be able to determine this by the soil line on the bark. Spread the roots carefully and cover with a few inches of good soil, packing firmly with your foot or a blunt stick.

Fill the hole with water to cover this and work the mud around the roots to fill all air pockets. Let the water settle, fill the rest of the hole and repeat the process of packing, soaking and puddling. When the filling of the hole is completed, leave a slight depression to catch rainfall.

The care of newly-planted trees the first summer is of utmost importance for they must overcome the shock of transplanting. To prevent damage to the bark that is known as "sun scald," any newly planted tree that is one inch or more thick at the base should be wrapped with burlap, heavy paper or aluminum foil for protection from the sun. Sometimes I slit a length of old rubber hose down one side and use this as a wrapping, securing

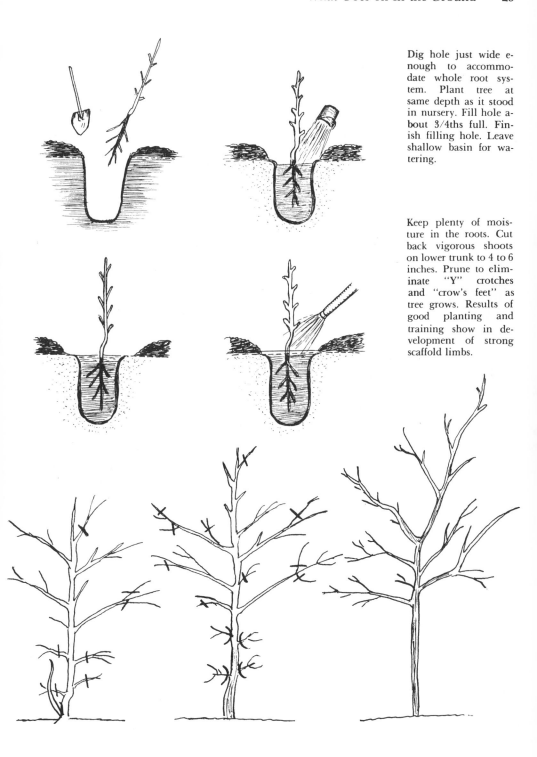

Dig hole just wide e-nough to accommo-date whole root sys-tem. Plant tree at same depth as it stood in nursery. Fill hole a-bout 3/4ths full. Fin-ish filling hole. Leave shallow basin for wa-tering.

Keep plenty of mois-ture in the roots. Cut back vigorous shoots on lower trunk to 4 to 6 inches. Prune to elim-inate "Y" crotches and "crow's feet" as tree grows. Results of good planting and training show in de-velopment of strong scaffold limbs.

it at top and bottom, but not too tightly. With a whip or severely pruned tree, leave only the top few buds protruding. But if your tree is branched, wrap the entire trunk up to the lowest branch. Keep it wrapped during the first two summers but be sure to loosen the wrapping to avoid strangulation as the trunk grows.

Here, I'd like to mention something that's forgotten all too often. If a tree tag is attached with a bit of wire, be sure to remove it. It may seem loose at the time, but as the tree grows and leaves hide the branch from view the wire may tighten into the tree, cutting off circulation and strangling the limb.

When you have finished with planting and wrapping, place a mulch of peat, straw, compost, lawn clippings or leaves for about three feet around the tree to conserve moisture and keep the roots cool in hot weather.

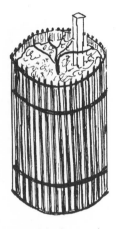

Cylindrical matting screen arrangement.

In a lawn area you may wish to remove this mulch after the first season for the sake of looks, but I do not advise it. A low, neat fence a few feet from the trunk of your tree will help to keep the mulch from spreading on the lawn and still will allow the tree the nourishment it needs.

In an orchard or fence-row planting this need not be so much a consideration. As suggested before, you can leave the mulch on permanently, adding more each year and extending it outward with the growth of the tree.

Supplemental watering is of utmost importance during the first years while the new taproot is forming and taking hold. The soil should never become completely dried out during this period. However, daily watering is not advised, since you may drown the tree with so much water that air never has a chance to penetrate into the soil at all.

Burlap Screen

Horizontal screening.

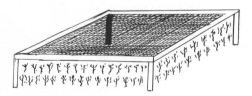

IF YOU BUY BAREROOT TREES

Many times and for many reasons it is just not possible to buy trees from a local nurseryman and have them delivered to your property already balled and burlapped. Often to obtain the exact variety you want to plant, it must come from a long distance. This has grown increasingly expensive, so that many nurseries prefer to ship their trees "bareroot" when they are dormant. They consider this easier, less expensive and actually safer for the trees.

A nurseryman told me how he does this, and the care he suggested on arrival: "We prune the roots very little, for it is the tiny, hair-like roots that supply nourishment while the heavier roots supply the stability. Staking the tree when it is planted will benefit the tree by giving these roots a chance to grow and hold the trees steady. Roots are sometimes snapped off due to heavy winds if the tree is not supported, and it dies without the owner every being aware that this has happened.

"We take care also to cut off any damaged roots before shipment, but they should be inspected again upon arrival and any that were damaged in transit removed.

"Trees should be unpacked as soon as possible after arrival (providing the package is not frozen — in which case let the trees thaw out in a cool room for several days before unpacking), and the roots placed in a pail of water. If, due to delays in transportation, the trees seem exceptionally dry, lay them their entire length in water for several hours or overnight before planting. Use the bathtub for this if you have nothing else.

"Keep the trees in a pail of water while transporting to the planting site, or enclose the roots in a plastic or burlap bag. When the hole is ready, remove and plant at once. Be sure to plant only one tree at a time, covering the roots well and watering before starting another."

I'll note the planting distances for nut trees separately with each variety, for they vary. It also will depend on what you expect from your trees. Orchard plantings should be spaced carefully and correctly for best results, but in the lawn or limited area of a home orchard they may be planted much closer together.

Perhaps I should mention that the Black Walnut has been found toxic to a few other types of plants. Some authorities believe this toxicity lies in the roots where they come in contact

Have your nut tree and flowers, too.

with such plants. Others say that the Black Walnut releases a substance called "juglone," which is washed from its leaves and causes incompatibility. Perhaps both are right. Cultivated plants that are not compatible with Black Walnuts are apples, alfalfa, potatoes, tomatoes and blackberries.

While it is believed that the Butternut shares some of the same toxic qualities, it has been proven that the Persian or English Walnut does not, and neither do any of the other generally planted nut trees that I know of.

While many species of nuts, such as the Pecan, are just as tasty in seed-grown trees (though usually smaller and harder to shell), you can count on grafted trees to bear younger. Do not, however, let this be a matter of major concern. It is far more important to work toward the development of a sturdy tree (whether native or grafted) capable of producing a good crop when fully developed, than to worry about a handful of nuts when the tree is only two or three years old.

Pollination of nut trees may pose a problem in a small planting unless other trees of the same type are located nearby, possibly in a neighbor's yard. The male flower appears in the form of a catkin that sheds its pollen in the spring. The female flower appears at the end of a small nutlet which must open during the pollen-shedding period in order to be fertilized. On some trees the two flower forms open simultaneously, but if pollen sheds at the wrong time, it is helpful to have others close enough for the wind to aid in fertilization. Catkins may be damaged over winter or by late spring frosts on one tree, but another may be intact. It also happens sometimes that a tree will produce catkins for a year or two before it produces nutlets.

All varieties of Filberts are self-unfertile and require a second variety nearby so the interchange of pollen can fertilize both plants. And the planting of a third variety may well increase your crop by introducing a greater supply of pollen at the necessary time.

The western soft-shelled Almonds, even though they may be hardy and make a lovely tree, will not bear in cold climates. They bloom too early and the frost kills the blossoms. But the hard-shelled Almonds will grow and produce anywhere that a Peach tree will thrive. They will bear a reasonable crop of nuts if planted alone, but since they are closely related to the Peach they will give a much heavier crop when fertilized by Peaches blooming at the same time.

So far I've said nothing in this chapter about Peanuts which, of course, do not come under the heading of nut trees at all. But, since they are nearly always considered along with nuts — though properly classed as a vegetable and belonging to the legume family — I think they have a place in this book. The protein and vitamin content of the Peanut is much the same as the nuts that grow on trees, and they are also used in cooking for much the same purposes.

Moreover, you can raise several crops of Peanuts and enjoy them while you are waiting for your nut trees to bear. While your trees are young and before they begin to offer too much shade, you can grow Peanuts right along with them in your nut orchard. All things being so much in their favor, I'm going to "include them in."

PRINCIPAL NUTS OF NORTH AMERICA

Variety	Years To Bear	Ultimate Height	Planting Distance	Range	Pollination	Nutritional Value
Almonds (Hardy)	2 to 4	15 to 25 ft.	25 ft.	Plant where Peaches grow	Two varieties Bee pollinated	Vitamins B¹ and A
Butternut (grafted)	3 to 5	40 to 50 ft.	40 ft.	All regions		Rich in protein
Butternut (seedlings)	1 to 14	40 to 50 ft.	40 ft.	All regions		Low in starch
Chestnut, Chinese	3 to 5	40 to 50 ft.	40 ft.	South	Two varieties or seedlings needed	Chestnuts starchy, chinkapin very nutritious
Filbert	2 to 4	8 to 10 ft.	15 ft.	Pacific northwest	Two varieties needed	Hazels starchy, contain vitamin C
Hickory (grafted) shagbark shellbark	5 to 7	60 to 80 ft.	40 ft.	North and Middle West Great Plains	Two varieties needed	Protein, carbohydrates & Vitamin C
Pecan (grafted)	4 to 6	60 to 80 ft.	50 ft.	Plant where peaches grow	Two varieties needed	Vitamins A and B²
Pecan (seedlings)	15 to 18	60 to 80 ft.	50 ft.	Plant where peaches grow	Two varieties needed	Vitamins A and B²
Black walnut (grafted)	3 to 5	80 to 100 ft.	60 ft.	most all regions	Two varieties needed	Vitamins C, A, B¹ and B²
Heartmut	4 to 5	50 to 60 ft.	40 ft.	most all regions	Two varieties needed	Vitamins C, A, B¹ and B²
Black walnuts (seedlings)	15 to 18	80 to 100 ft.	60 ft.	All regions	Two varieties needed	
English walnut (grafted) Carpathian	4 to 5	60 to 70 ft.	40 ft.	All regions	Two varieties needed. Or mate with Blacks	High in calcium Vitamins A, B¹, B²
English Walnut (seedlings)	7 to 12	60 to 70 ft.	40 ft.	All regions		Vitamins B² & B¹
Peanut	First season	18 to 20 in.	Space 1 foot apart in row	All regions	Blossoms bee pollinated	Vitamins E in oil

3

GRAFTING
AND BUDDING

Changing a native nut tree into one of known performance can be a source of great pleasure and satisfaction, not only in the results obtained but in the actual procedure as well. It's fun!

Here are some of the reasons why the grafting of nut trees is widely practiced: Seeds do not produce trees true to variety; each native tree may be a variety all its own; some trees are difficult to reproduce by cuttings; better pollinating varieties may be needed to improve the set of nuts in a grove situation.

Some years ago experiments were made here in Oklahoma grafting Pecan wood to Hickory stock. It didn't work out well. The grafts started out into good growth but suddenly stopped and then died. Graft Hickories to Hickories and Pecans to Pecans. Even though the two trees are related species, "to each his own" is a good rule to follow.

Of course all nut trees are not *exactly* alike, and individual differences will be noted in succeeding chapters, but in general the rules given here for grafting and budding will apply to most trees.

SPLICE AND TONGUE GRAFTING

The splice and tongue graft (sometimes called whip graft) is very useful — particularly for propagating small seedling trees and branches of larger trees. The best time to graft is from February to early April, depending on your climate, before growth starts.

You will need a sharp knife, masking tape and some orange shellac.

Use dormant one-year-old graftwood (the scion). The diameter of the scion and stock (the tree or branch) should be as nearly as possible the same size to assure maximum contact. The best size is three-eighths to three-quarters of an inch diameter, but one-inch stocks and scions have been used successfully.

Each scion should contain at least two buds and be about six inches long. Small trees should be grafted near the ground line to reduce maintenance.

1. First cut off the tree trunk or branch where you'll attach the graft by making a long, straight, sloping cut. The face of the cut should be two or three inches long. Try to make the cut with one stroke of the knife.

2. To make the tongue, start a cut about a third of the distance from the tip of the cut-off tree and press the knife slowly downward (being careful not to split) about two-thirds the length of the bevel cut on the trunk. Do not loosen the bark.

3. Make a similar, sloping cut on the basal or bigger end of the scion. Hold the the scion wood in one hand and cut by pushing the blade away from your body.

4. Make the tongue cut on the scion in the same manner as on the trunk or stock.

5. Match the parts together. If the two parts are not quite the same size, be sure to make contact between the inner bark on one side and the lower end of the graft. If the cuts are made properly, the stock and scion will appear as one.

6. Wrap the union tightly with masking tape, special grafting tape or polyethelene budding tape to exclude air and hold the union firmly together. Cover the taped area with orange shellac to prevent excessive moisture loss.

When two-year-old scion wood is used, new shoot growth may be delayed as much as three weeks, but growth will be very rapid when it starts. After vigorous scion growth begins, the more durable tapes should be cut to prevent girdling.

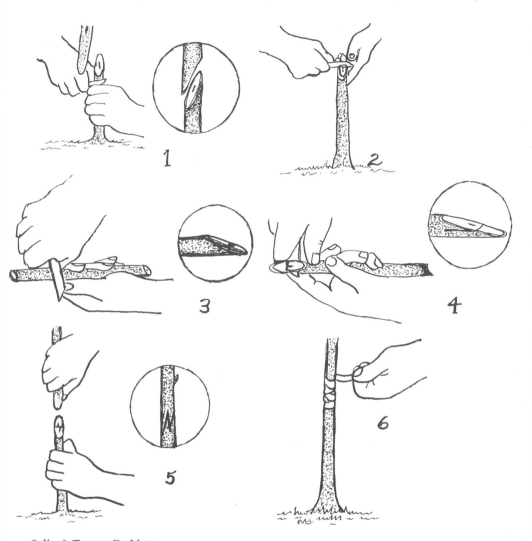

Splice & Tongue Grafting

1. To cut off branch or trunk, make a long, straight, sloping cut (two to three inches long) with one stroke of the knife.

2. For the tongue, start your cut about a third the distance from the tip of the cut-off tree. Press the knife slowly downward, being careful not to split, about two-thirds the length of the bevel cut on the trunk. Take care not to loosen the bark.

3. Now make a similar sloping cut on the basal end of the scion. Hold the scion wood in one hand and cut by pushing the blade away.

4. The tongue cut on the scion is made in the same manner in the stock.

5. The parts should match. If not quite the same size, try to make contact between the inner bark on one side and the lower end of the graft. Done properly the stock and scion will appear as one.

6. Union now should be tightly wrapped with special grafting tape to exclude air and hold the joint firmly. Cover taped area with orange shellac.

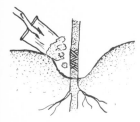

Some nurserymen prefer to remove 4 to 6 inches of soil from around the stock. Then replace the soil and firm around the tree, covering the entire taped area.

Nurserymen produce stocks for grafting by planting nuts three or four inches apart in rows. They usually graft the young trees at the beginning of the second or third year's growth. Vigorous trees are selected three-eighths to three-quarters of an inch in diameter (at six to twelve inches above the ground) and spaced eight to twelve inches apart. Excess trees are removed to provide room for rapid growth. Then the trees will be ready for digging and transplanting the following season.

Some nurserymen remove four to six inches of soil from the stock with a disc plow and/or a hoe. The graft is made at or below the original soil level, and the soil then is replaced and firmed around the tree, covering the entire taped area. During extremely dry seasons, the soil must be moistened until growth is well under way.

If you have planted several nuts where a permanent tree location is wanted, select the best seedling tree and remove the least desirable ones at the end of the first growing season. After one or two more growing seasons the selected seedling tree may be converted to an improved variety with a splice and tongue graft outlined earlier.

If you have young native or seedling trees such as Pecans or Walnuts growing in a good field or pasture location, they can be propagated to improved varieties. Splice and tongue grafts can be made on the central leaders at whatever height is necessary to accommodate the size of the propagation wood. Remember to follow through with proper maintenance, such as removal of native sprouts, cutting the tape, and in some instances staking the tree.

PATCH BUDDING

Patch budding may be done on small tree trunks or branches that are three-eighths to one-and-a-half inches in diameter. Larger trees that have been cut back also may be patch budded by placing the bud on young vigorous sprouts forced into growth near the cut end of the limbs. Trees cut back in one dormant season may be patch budded in the spring of the following season.

For most nut trees the patch budding technique is best when used in the spring or late summer. Budwood which has grown during the previous growing season is used in spring. It is

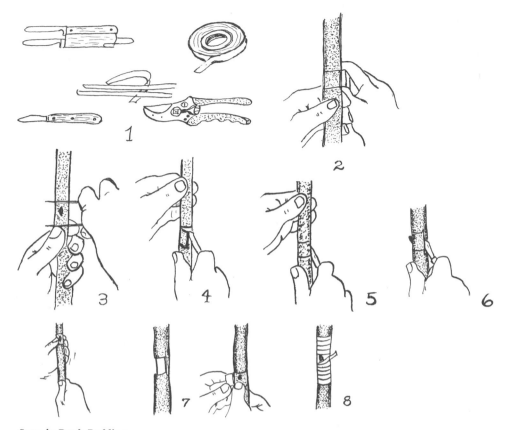

Steps in Patch Budding

1. Tools needed: sharp, twin-bladed knife; polyethylene or masking tape or rubber budding strips; hand shears; sharp single-blade knife.

2. Select a smooth location on stock and make a double cut about 1½ inches long by rotating double-bladed knife around stock.

3. Now double-cut the budwood. Choose a plump, healthy bud and center it between blades of knife. Using firm pressure, begin on left side of bud and rotate knife to right. Make the double cut through the bark and about 1½ inches long.

4. Complete work on the stock by connecting double cut on the right side with one perpendicular cut, using single-bladed knife.

5. Raise the bark on the stock with flip of knife point.

6. Connect the double cut on both sides of the bud with two perpendicular cuts. Loosen patch containing bud at all four corners with knife point. Hold bud patch between left thumb and index finger. Twist left hand, with right hand rotating budstick in opposite direction.

7. When completely loose, pick up patch and bud between knife and thumb and quickly place in matrix on the stock, even with the right side of connecting cut made on the stock. Now crease the bark flap on the stock and tear or cut to fit the patch. A slight overlap of the bark flap over the patch can remain.

8. Use plastic budding tape, rubber strips or masking tape to seal the patch. Pull wraps firmly, allowing them to overlap slightly. All exposed areas should be well covered and the bud show through the wraps.

collected in late winter (February or early March) while the trees are dormant, and is kept in cold storage until budding season. Here in Oklahoma the current season's buds usually are sufficiently mature and available for patch budding by the middle of July.

The two seasons for budding vary from each other as follows:

SPRING BUDDING

The bark of dormant budwood must be seasoned to induce slipping. This can be done by removing the budwood from cold storage four or five days before it is to be used and leaving it, at room temperature, in the storage container or in moist packing material.

However, where trees of the desired varieties are located nearby, two-year-old wood usually contains dormant buds as late as May or early June if the trees are vigorous. These buds can be removed and used for patch budding at that time. This alternative procedure to spring budding has the advantage of eliminating the collection and storing of dormant budwood in late summer and the artificial slipping of the bark.

LATE SUMMER BUDDING

Current growth is used here. Dispose of the leaf stalk which is found immediately below each bud. Precautions always should be taken (from the time the first cuts are made until wrapped) not to expose the wounds to sunlight or wind any longer than absolutely necessary. Keep the budwood wrapped in a damp material such as burlap to prevent drying. Handle the budwood carefully, avoiding unnecessary rubbing, bruising or splitting of the patch containing the bud. Two or three weeks after insertion of the bud, determine if the patchbud is green by nicking it lightly with a knife point.

Good judgment is required at this stage to determine whether to force the live buds now or the following spring. Buds inserted by mid-June and well united to the stock are commonly forced the same season. Others may be forced the following spring.

To force transplanted buds, cut off the stock six or eight inches above the bud. This "stub" will serve as a support to which the young shoot arising from the bud can be tied. Do not allow growth to develop on this section of the stock during the first growing season. At the end of the first growing season the stock can be cut off smooth, immediately above the new shoot.

Durable wrapping materials may need to be released after the wound of the budding operation has healed, and under good growing conditions this will be about three weeks after budding. Cut the tape or other wrapping material with a knife blade on the back side of the stock, opposite the transplanted bud.

BARK GRAFTING

Bark grafting involves transferring a shoot containing one or more buds from one tree to another in such a way that a union is formed and a new top is produced. The formation of callus between the stock and scion is necessary for growth of the bud, callus being the soft tissue which forms over any wounded or cut surface of a stem.

Selecting the best variety to propagate is very important. If scab disease, for instance, is prevalent in your area, choose a disease-resistant variety. Consider the length of your growing season, and remember that elevation also limits the use of some varieties. Propagation wood of suitable varieties can be secured from several sources. There is a list in the back of book, or ask your county agent.

This modified inlay bark grafting is one of the most convenient methods of top-working some native trees such as Pecans. It is done during early spring soon after the bark will slip. Early setting of scions is best, but bark grafting may be done successfully during May if the scions are kept properly dormant in cold storage and are set before they have dried out or warmed up enough for the bark to start slipping.

The bark on the stock must be slipping, but that on the scion must be tight. Use dormant scions cut during the winter and kept in cold storage. The cambium layers (the soft cellular tissue between bark and wood, and from which new bark and new wood originate) of the stock and scion are brought in contact to prevent drying out, while the union is being made. After this an entirely new top of the tree grows from the scion.

The tools you will need for this work are:

Saw: Small sturdy, coarse-toothed, with plenty of set.

Hand Shears: Sturdy but lightweight, for cutting grafts the proper length.

Knife: Sturdy, large handle, holds edge well.

Whetstone: For keeping knife sharp.

Small Hammer: Lightweight for driving nails.

Nails: Flathead No. 18, five-eights to three-quarters inch long.

Carpenter's Apron: A convenient carrier for holding equipment.

Aluminum foil, polyethylene bags, orange shellac, brush, rubber bands and string.

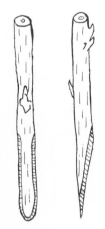

1. The Stock

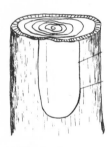

2. The Scion

PROCEDURE FOR BARK GRAFTING

Select young, sturdy trees located a suitable distance from each other, according to variety.

Prepare stock by sawing it off at convenient height to work, usually four to six feet high if the area is in pasture. The best size tree to graft is one to four inches in diameter where the scion is to be set. It is advisable to leave a side branch within six to eight inches of the top if it is available. Remove rough bark only on the stock as indicated in Figure 1. Make the smoothed area just large enough to accommodate the scion.

Select and prepare a scion as indicated in Figure 2. Cut the scion square across its top and on its bottom end make the sloping cut two or more inches long. Remove a thin layer of outside bark on both sides of the sloping cut and across the point as indicated. Avoid any delay in making the graft. Do not allow the exposed area of the graft to dry out. Keep your hands from touching the exposed area.

Place prepared scion on smooth area of stock as indicated in Figure 3. Make a pattern cut along the sides of scion into which the scion will fit exactly. Work quickly with your back toward the sun to form a shade while preparing the graft. About one inch below the top of stock, in center of pattern, score the bark slightly part way through the cambium to secure a better fit as shown in Figure 4.

Loosen this bark flap at top to insert the point of scion under bark, as indicated in Figure 4 and force downward into place. This forces the flap of bark out of the slot. Leave about one-sixteenth inch of the cut on the scion showing above the stock on the bark side.

Cut off about half of the bark flap and nail the scion firmly to the stock, as indicated in Figure 5, with the flatheaded No. 18 nails, their length depending on size of scion. Use a small hammer to avoid damaging the graft.

Use aluminum foil, bright side out, and wrap the upper eight inches of the stock, covering the top also (see Figure 6), permitting the foil to extend upon the scion "graft" about one-half inch, pressing the foil firmly with the fingers until it stays in place. A piece of foil 8 x 12 inches usually is enough.

Clip the corner of a quart-size polyethylene bag and place it over the stock with the graft extending out through the corner. Use a rubber band, medium size, to tie around the graft, securing the corner of the bag. A small amount of the aluminum foil may be involved also at the base of the scion, as in Figure 7.

Fold the bag around the stock and tie it with string to prevent blowing off. Cover the top of scion and down to the plastic area with orange shellac. Remember to remove the durable string that is holding the foil in place about July 1. Often it is a good practice to nail a support to the newly grafted tree to help protect the rapidly-growing graft from blowing out.

8. Sealing

7. Bagging Top

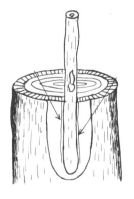

3. Fitting Stock to Scion

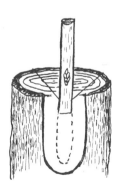

4. Scion Pattern

5. Nailing Scion

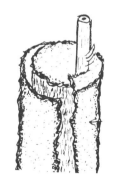

6. Wrapping

4

THE PEERLESS PECAN

The Pecan is the oldest nut tree native cultivated in America, and it may have been the only native tree planted by the American Indians before the white man came. It grows wild in Louisiana, Oklahoma, Texas and the Mississippi Valley but now is cultivated widely in other parts of the United States.

Many improved varieties introduced include the *Starking Hardy Giant Paper Shell* Pecan, an extremely hardy tree that has survived winters of 20 degrees below zero and still has produced. The large nuts, often over one-and-a half inches long, ripen in early September in Zone 6. This means that it can be grown as far north as some parts of Washington state and southern New York.

The many good southern paper shell Pecans, include the *Schley*, which is considered by many the most beautiful of this type. Another general favorite is the *Stuart*, probably the most widely grown of all. This vigorous tree is highly regarded as a big producer of large-size nuts with easily cracked thin shells. The plump, flavorful kernels separate perfectly from the shell. Other named varieties popular in the southern states include

Burkett, Graking, Hayes, Mahan, Moneymaker, Nugget, Patrick, San Saba Improved, Success, Texas, Western, USDA Varieties Apache, Barton, Choctaw, Comanche, Mohawk, Sioux, Wichita, Major and *Peruque.* Each of these is characterized by certain qualities which make it a good choice for either commercial or home garden production, according to the section of the country where a planting is to be made.

Some varieties are desirable because they mature late or early, some for their ease of hulling (a thin shell making them easy to crack) others for their disease-resistance and still others for their abundant bearing. Good flavor also is a quality of utmost importance. Some of these Pecans have been developed by selectively choosing the best nuts from native trees, some represent careful varietal crosses and others have come from choice seedlings in test planting.

In addition to grafted Pecans, many nurseries now offer good seedling trees from selected nuts of proven worth. One of these is the *Missouri Hardy Seedling Pecan* (Stark Bros.), the hardiest tree they offer, and which may be planted even in areas considered unfavorable to Pecan trees, in the colder Northern sections. The medium-large nuts are rich and highly flavored, and the trees bear young and regularly. They may be grown in Zones 5 to 9, which includes some areas of Michigan, Wisconsin and Montana and on southward to Florida and Texas.

By now you know that for flavor and texture I lean just a little toward high class, large, good quality native Pecans. So if you live in the North and cannot grow paper shell grafted varieties you really don't need to feel badly about it. On the other hand, this is just my own personal opinion, and there is now such a wide choice among the grafted varieties that there surely is a Pecan somewhere that will suit just about everybody.

If you choose to purchase one of the good grafted varieties, by all means do so. If you decide to buy selected seedling trees, that's fine too. But if you want to plant seeds and grow your own, here's how:

PROPAGATION BY SEED

Although many nut trees do not bear fruits true to variety when propagated by seeds, it is necessary to plant the seeds in order to get the understock on which to propagate the wood of better varieties. And, in order to get the seeds to germinate, certain treatments need to be given.

The seeds of nut trees, having a hard seed coat, may be treated by one of three methods in order to make the seed coats permeable to water.

(1) soaking in sulfuric acid.

(2) soaking in hot water, or immersing seed for a short period in boiling water.

(3) mechanical scarification.

The major problem, however, is dormancy of the embryo. Of all the causes of natural delay in seed germination "dormancy of the embryo" is most common. Seed with a dormant embryo must complete a process of "after-ripening" before it acquires the ability to germinate. After-ripening takes place only at the proper temperature and in the presence of abundant supplies of moisture and air (oxygen). Now, while this applies to the seeds of most Hickories which are dormant (requiring stratification described shortly for various periods of time depending on species), and to Black Walnuts (whose seeds are shed from the tree in a dormant state), Pecans are different.

Pecans do *not* fall into dormancy, but can germinate at any time when conditions are favorable. Remember I told you I frequently find them coming up in my garden where they are turned under with the leaves to a shallow depth.

Nevertheless, despite this difference, Pecan seed is commonly stratified or kept in cold storage at high humidity through the winter so it can be planted in the spring of the year. This type of winter storage prevents the nut from getting rancid and losing its viability and, at the same time, it excludes the possibility of germination too soon out of season. If planted during the fall or winter, the Pecan, not being dormant, usually will germinate the next spring. You see how easily you can have a shade tree, a windbreak or a grove?

Pecans do best, when planted primarily for nut production, on deep fertile and moist yet well-drained soils. Low areas that get a bit more than their share of water often produce better crops. However, Pecans are adaptable and will grow under a wide range of conditions.

All Pecans are started from planted nuts and, not being dormant, they may be planted in the fall, winter or spring. Select for planting large nuts that are mature and well-filled. Little advantage has been found in selecting nuts from any one variety since none will produce true to kind. This, of course, in particular applies to nuts from grafted trees. I have noticed that large, thin-shelled natives *do* tend to produce a large proportion of seedling trees that will bear nuts similar to the parent tree.

STRATIFY OR SOAK PECAN NUTS

In preparing the nuts for planting, it is considered best to place them in alternate, two inch layers with moist sand or sawdust in a wooden box (such as an apple box). This box should be buried underground sometime during the winter in a well-drained place and left until spring. It is a good idea to place a piece of hardware cloth over the top of the box to prevent pilfering by rodents — if you suspect their presence in the vicinity. If the ground freezes it will not injure the nuts.

In the spring the nuts are removed and planted about 10 inches apart and three inches deep in wide rows, or they may be planted three to the hill at locations where you want your tree to remain permanently. Be sure to place a stake or marker at each hill.

Although planting may be made any time from fall through early April, early-planted nuts sometimes are destroyed by rodents, and that is the reason for stratifying the nuts in wet sand or sawdust or other suitable materials for planting in late spring. February would be the best time for planting in southern regions, a little later in the North.

Another treatment for dry nuts, to hasten and aid in their germination, is to soak them in water five to seven days just before spring planting.

Your Pecan trees grow very slowly for the first two or three years, but during this time a long tap root may extend downward four feet or more. When more than one tree is growing in a hill, select the best one and destroy the others. I like to pull them up when they and their tap roots still are quite small, since if the unwanted trees are just cut off they will send up another top, and cutting must be repeated several times.

Young pecan trees three-eights to three-quarters inches in diameter may be propagated to improved varieties by splice grafting, or patch or chip budding. Or the trees can be bark grafted when eight to 10 feet high. Young trees in the nursery row usually are splice grafted the second or third year and allowed to grow another year or two before they are dug for transplanting. The first successful propagating of Pecans by grafting, incidentally, was done in Louisiana in 1845. The gardener is known to us only by the name of Antoine.

PECAN VARIETIES (GRAFTED SOUTHERN TYPES)

	Harvest Season	Scab Resistance	Precosi
Barton	Mid	Good	Good
Caddo	Mid	Fair	Good
Cape Fear	Early	Fair	Good
Choctaw	Mid-Late	Fair	Fair
Curtis	Late	Good	Fair
Desirable	Mid-Late	Good	Fair
Elliott	Mid	Good	Fair
Farley	Mid	Poor	Fair
Harris Super	Mid-Late	Fair	Good
Hastings	Late	Good	Poor
Kernodle	Mid-Late	Fair	Fair
Mahan	Mid	Poor	Fair
Mahan-Stuart	Mid	Poor	Fair
Moneymaker	Early	Fair	Fair
Moore	Early	Poor	Fair
Moreland	Mid	Fair	Fair
Cluster	Early	Good	Fair
Schley	Mid	Poor	Poor
Stuart	Mid	Fair	Poor
Success	Mid	Poor	Fair
Wichita	Mid-Late	Poor	Good

Ease of cracking	Percentage Kernel	Kernel quality	Pollination**
Fair	Fair	Fair	Good overlap
Fair	Good	Good	Protandrous
Good	Fair	Fair	Protandrous
Fair	Good	Good	Protogynous
Good	Good	Good	Protogynous
Good	Good	Good	Protandrous
Fair	Good	Good	Protogynous
Good	Fair	Fair	Protandrous
Fair	Fair	Fair	Protogynous
Good	Fair	Fair	Protandrous
Good	Fair	Good	?
Good	Poor	Fair	Protogynous
Good	Poor	Fair	Protogynous
Fair	Fair	Fair	Protogynous
Fair	Fair	Fair	Protandrous
Good	Fair	Good	?
Fair	Fair	Fair	?
Good	Good	Good	Protogynous
Poor	Fair	Fair	Protogynous
Fair	Fair	Fair	Protandrous
Good	Good	Good	Protogynous

*Precocity refers to the age when a tree begins to bear. A good precocious variety normally will bear a few nuts the fourth year.

**With a protandrous variety the pollen (male) is mature most years before the stigma (female) is receptive. With a protogynous variety, the stigma is receptive most years before the pollen is mature. It is desirable to interplant protandrous and protogynous varieties.

HARDY GRAFTED PECAN TREES FOR THE NORTH

Variety	Size	Flavor
Perugue	Medium	Excellent
Major	Medium	Excellent
Colby	Medium large	Very good
Posey	Medium	Very good
Giles	Medium	Good
Hodge	Medium large	Very good
Green River	Medium large	Very good
Chief	Largest	Excellent
Patrick	Medium	Good
J. Ford	Medium	Very good

TRANSPLANTING PECAN TREES

Because of their long tap roots Pecans present problems slightly different from other nut trees, and it is considered difficult to get transplants to live through the first summer. February, March or early April is the best time to transplant the trees in southern states — a little later further north.

Although four to five-foot trees are considered by many to be the best size for transplanting, better livability often is achieved when thrifty one-year-old propagation trees are used. Select the varieties best adapted for your section.

Because of the long tap root it is advisable to use a power posthole digger (12 or 14 inches in diameter) if a number of trees are to be planted. Dig the hole deep enough to accommodate the root system of the tree to be planted. The tap root will usually be from two-and-a-half to four feet in length. Set the tree about one inch deeper than it grew in the nursery row. The Pecan tree is dormant at transplanting time, but it is extremely important to prevent drying out during or after setting. Damp burlap or other suitable covering should be used while planting to prevent damage to the tree roots from exposure to sun or wind.

Cracking	Bearing	No. of Yrs.
Excellent	Thinner shell	3 to 5 Years
Excellent	Prolific	Early 3 to 5 Years
Excellent	Very prolific	3 to 5 Years
Very good	Very good	5 to 7 Years
Very good	Prolific	3 to 5 Years
Very good	Prolific	5 to 7 Years
Very good	Good in southern states as well	3 to 5 Years
Very good	Fair	3 to 5 Years
Very good	Good	3 to 5 Years
Excellent	Data not yet available	Data not yet available

(a) Place the tree in the hole to make sure that it is deep enough.

(b) Trim off the ends of all broken roots. Do *not* twist the tree around to make it fit the hole.

(c) Fill in around the tree roots with the moist top soil.

(d) Settle the soil with a suitable tamper until the hole is three-quarters full.

(e) Next, water to settle soil around the tree roots.

(f) Finish filling the hole, and leave the soil loose at the surface.

(g) Remove about one-half of the top of the transplanted tree.

(h) Wrap the tree trunk from the ground up 18 to 24 inches or within about six inches of the top, to prevent sunscald, drying out, insect attacks and injury from rabbits. Use special wrapping material for this purpose or heavy brown paper, burlap or aluminum foil.

During the first summer it is necessary to water the trees if the soil becomes dry, but do not over-water especially when newly transplanted. Turn to later pages for more details on watering. Clean cultivation of the soil near the trunk at this time will enable the trees to grow faster.

Pecan trees will grow to a very large size if conditions are favorable. This should be allowed for when the varieties are selected and the planting pattern is developed for a grove, and it also should be a consideration for home planting.

When a Pecan grove is being established, 30 to 40 feet spacing is best for the first 15 to 20 years. After crowding starts, the trees will require thinning to a spacing of 60 to 80 feet. Remember, when it is necessary to thin a grove, that Pecan timber is one of the most valuable woods.

Pecan trees are available from a number of reliable nurseries, and the important thing to consider when buying them is to secure field-fresh dug trees. Poor results will occur usually with trees that have been held in storage for long periods of time. If the bundle of nursery trees appears dry when you receive it, open it at once and soak the trees in cool water overnight or several hours prior to planting.

POLLINATION REQUIREMENTS

Pecan trees are monoecious (having both male and female flowers on the same tree). The male flowers are three-branched catkins produced on last year's wood. The pollen is carried by the wind to the female flowers, which are borne in clusters on the current season's growth. While most Pecan varieties are considered self-fruitful, better production is obtained when more than one variety is planted.

Wet weather during the pollination period may reduce the dissemination of pollen. So it's a good plan to leave a few native Pecan trees in the vicinity of the grove to furnish additional pollen. Some native trees bear their pollen early and others late. Pollination is completed most years usually during the last days of May.

The tip ends of the nutlets turn brown and harden immediately after they are pollinized or their receptive period is passed. If the female flower fails to receive pollen it usually turns yellow and falls to the ground within a week or so.

According to Dr. G.W. Adriance, head of the Horticulture Department of Texas A & M College, three-quarters of the small nut drop that usually occurs in June (or about six weeks after the pollination period), is a result of the female flowers not becoming fertilized.

There is no evidence of cross-incompatibility in Pecan varieties which have been tested. Instead the problem develops because the male and female flowers do not mature at the same time. *Moore, Texas Prolific* and *San Saba* have pollen available in time to pollinate the earliest flowers of any variety. *Moneymaker* and *Success* usually depend upon other varieties for pollination. *Stuart, Burkett, Schley* and *Delmas* sometimes require pollen from other varieties.

WHAT TO LOOK FOR IN PECAN VARIETIES

Any time two Pecan growers get together you can expect the subject of Pecan varieties to be thoroughly debated. But experience over the years has taught growers that newly-introduced varieties in time may prove not as well adapted as they first appeared. Environment is a very big factor in satisfactory performance, so choose trees adapted to your section or area.

In deciding upon the selection of a variety here are some points that should be taken into consideration. The tree should be:

Fruitful: (a) Bear heavy annual crops, (b) Start producing at an early age, (c) Mature the nuts before frost.
Disease Resistant: To scab and leaf diseases.
Hardy: (a) Winter hardy, (b) Escape late spring frosts.
Have Good Growth Habits: (a) Large, dense foliage, (b) Retain foliage until frost, (c) Good branching traits.
The nuts should be:
In Size: (a) Brittle and thin enough to shell easily, yet, (b) Tough enough not to split during harvest.
In Shelling Quality: (a) Yield 50 percent or more kernels, (b) Shells separate easily from the kernels, (c) Large percent of whole kernels. (Long-shaped nuts crack best.)
In Kernel Quality: (a) Firm, plump, light-bright yellow color, (b) Good flavor, taste, high oil content.

IMPROVING NATIVE GROVES

In areas where Pecans grow wild they are often found along creeks and rivers where they are crowded by oak, elm and other trees and by underbrush. This competition for moisture and fertility often results in low yields, sometimes even to the point of making it uneconomical to harvest the crop.

Removal of the excess trees may be done by several methods (depending on the local situation), such as by girdling, bulldozing and cutting. Even after all foreign timber has been removed many areas still may be too crowded with the Pecan trees. Thinning Pecans to the correct stand is a continuing process as the trees increase in size. Even so, it is best to remove trees only after the performance of each is known.

This is because each native tree is a variety all its own, with wide differences in production, size of nuts and nut quality. The percent of kernel which occurs in trees growing close to one another should be noted before trees are removed to obtain the desired spacing. Observations over a period of two or three years often are necessary before the right selections can be made. Forty to eighty feet or even more distance (depending upon the size of the trees), may be needed in order to allow space for wide, symmetrical top development.

Pecan trees properly spaced gradually will increase in production for several years, but additional thinning to keep the trees well spaced will be necessary as they grow. When the tree branches begin to touch, there is crowding, and thinning should be done.

But, proceed with caution. Wind breakage and sun scald may occur if all of the thinning is done at one time. Thin your trees over an extended period of time, allowing gradual adjustment to take place.

Some method of soil management should be adopted, too, as soon as clearing is completed in the grove; otherwise briars, brush and weeds will start to take over. On land where native groves have ample sunshine and adequate drainage, pasture can be provided for livestock. Groves that are cultivated with winter legume cover crops will produce more Pecans on the average, but the total income that includes livestock is often larger. Annual covers for the summer months work well, but permanent pasture grasses such as Bermuda should not be used in with Pecans since the competition for soil moisture during late summer is apt to be too severe.

In addition to improvement of mature stand of native trees, small Pecan trees less than four inches in diameter, that are found in the grove in good locations, may be grafted to improved varieties.

REMOVING SURPLUS TREES

The trees to be removed from the area often are suitable for saw timber, fence posts or firewood. Plan ahead by checking all available outlets, since timber sales made this way quite often can result in equaling the cost of clearing the area of excess trees. Fall and winter months are the best times to work in the timber. Be sure that all trees you have decided to remove have been plainly marked well ahead of this time.

THE NEED FOR SPACE

Older Pecan trees have been known to rise to the majestic height of 160 feet. The most needed practice in improving a grove is to provide sufficient space for each tree. This is the greatest single problem.

When branches touch, depend upon it, they are badly overcrowded. Other symptoms are small leaves, light green in color and early shedding of the leaves in the fall. Also look for short twig growth, shedding of the lower branches or irregular and low production of nuts.

To be productive Pecan trees need plenty of sunshine, fertile soil and sufficient soil moisture. Trees well spaced soon will give evidence of more plant food available, good care and management, and have the following advantages:

Having better health, foliage and growth, they are less subject to diseases. Each tree bears more nuts; the nuts often are larger and better filled; the trees withstand drought better; the nuts are easier to harvest; the trees are better shaped; have more bearing surface; the area can be used for cover crops and can be used for grazing livestock; easier use of machinery for spraying and harvesting; less danger of fire, predators and thieves where area is open.

How to Determine Space Needs by Tree Size		
Average Trunk Diameter Inches at 4 ft. height	Cross-Section Square Feet at 4 ft. height	Desirable Number Trees Per Acre
1-12	X	30
13.6	1	30
19.2	2	15
23.2	3	10
27.1	4	7 to 8
30.3	5	6

A total of 30 square feet of trunk cross-section is the maximum recommended for one acre.

USING PASTURE IN ORCHARDS

In many areas orchard pasturing of livestock is a common practice, and it may be done successfully with proper planning and management. Such a program will bring additional income from the land and often contributes greatly to good orchard management. Many pasture crops are soil-building and make excellent cover crops.

There is this to consider, too. It takes a fairly long time to grow a Pecan tree, and it usually grows on the best land of the farm, ranch or homestead.

The Pecan should be considered the *major* crop in a double cropping system because the production and yield of the nuts is determined by the condition and growth of the tree over a two-year period. Poor management of pasture during one season could damage two crops of nuts, and damaged trees are expensive either to repair or replace.

Shortages of plant food and moisture, or an excess of either during certain periods of the season, could cause a reduction in yield and poor nut quality. The ideal pasture crop for a Pecan orchard is soil-building in character. It does not compete with the trees for moisture or plant food and does not interfere with the harvesting of the nuts.

Winter annual pasture grasses and legumes fit these requirements best. These cover crops planted in the fall can be grazed out by June, before hot and dry weather starts. Such crops can be fertilized with phosphorous and potash and a little nitrogen in the fall and then top dressed with additional nitrogen in the spring as needed. The crop will not compete with the trees during the summer and the area will be clean for the nut harvest.

SELECTING PASTURE PLANTS

A combination of any of the small grains or annual rye grass, along with one or more annual winter legumes makes a good winter pasture for cattle. Here are some mixtures that could be used per acre of planting:

1. 50 lbs. rye and 30 to 40 lbs. winter oats with 15 lbs. vetch or crimson clover.
2. 40 lbs. rye or wheat and 40 lbs. barley with 10 lbs. vetch and 5 lbs. crimson clover.
3. 20 lbs. rye grass with 7 lbs. button clover or black medic. (In certain areas of Oklahoma where the soil is acid two lbs. of hop clover are recommended.)

Here again it is well to know the nature of your soil by having a test made, for there are combinations of grasses and legumes that may be most suitable for it. Small grains need well-drained soil; rye grows well on sandy soils. Vetch, crimson and hop clover will do well on the more acid soils. Button, black medic, the burr clovers and barley require sweeter soils.

FERTILIZER REQUIREMENTS

A full stand of bearing Pecan trees will use about as much fertilizer as a 50 bushel corn crop. Winter grasses, desirable though they are, use large amounts of nitrogen, and during the spring may have much of the available potash and phosphorous tied up. If this is suspected, again get a soil test, making sure that your tester knows the pasture is to be planted in a Pecan grove. Usually he will recommend about 50 percent additional fertilizer for the Pecans. Zinc is important (in spray form) in preventing rosette.

So far we have been mostly discussing Pecan orchards on a fairly large scale, but there are many people who would also like to grow Pecans on city lots. Here is the way the Agricultural Service in Texas advises such plantings be managed:

"For healthy, vigorous trees, high production and high quality of nuts it is essential that proper cultural practices be maintained. *Fertilizer, zinc,* and *water* are three very necessary elements in producing the type of vegetative growth necessary for a good harvest of nuts as well as maintaining an attractive tree. Never forget that leaves play an important part in producing quality nuts. And some 80 to 90 leaflets are required to develop and fill one medium size nut.

"Gauge your fertilization rate by the terminal growth made during the previous growing season. Healthy bearing trees should produce shoots 7 to 15 inches long. If terminal growth was less than 6 inches, increase the fertilization rate over the previous year. If the shoot growth exceeded 20 inches, reduce considerably the amount of fertilizer used. Very few nuts are produced on trees having terminal growth less than 6 or more than 20 inches.

"Bearing Pecan trees do not require large amounts of fertilizer, and a single application put on in late February or March is generally sufficient. Usually applying one-third pound of actual nitrogen per diameter inch of trunk will provide the terminal growth described above.

"Adjust your fertilization program each year to achieve the most favorable terminal growth. The home owner should also avoid using fertilizers containing weed killers because of the potential toxicity to trees.

"Pecans are deeply rooted trees but the majority of their absorptive 'feeder type roots' are within the upper 2 feet of soil. Thus, surface applications of fertilizer to the lawn area beneath the outer one-half to one-third of the tree canopy (drip line), followed by heavy watering, will work well. Rainfall during the late winter is usually sufficient to move the fertilizer into the root zone. Thus the lawn and Pecan trees are fertilized at the same time.

"Many home owners, however, still prefer to punch holes 12 to 15 inches deep and fill them with fertilizer. While this method works well, it requires more effort and has few advantages over the surface application.

WATCH FOR ZINC DEFICIENCY

"Pecans, particularly those growing in alkaline soils, are often very susceptible to zinc deficiency. This disorder, called 'rosette' is manifested as a chlorosis of leaves and dieback of shoots.

"The most reliable way of preventing or correcting rosette is by foliar spraying in the spring with zinc sulfate (two pounds per 100 gallons or about two tablespoons per gallon). This material should be included in the pesticide sprays used in April through early June. One yearly application is needed in all cases and two or three applications spaced three to four weeks apart are often best in many instances. Experience has shown that soil applications are seldom effective."

WATERING

The need for a dependable source of water for our nut and fruit trees once drove my husband and me to rather drastic steps. Years ago, before additional water supplies were found for our city, rationing often was necessary during the hot, dry months of summer. So we decided one spring to dig our own well to provide adequate water for our small orchard and the vegetable garden. Being young and agile in those days, possessing little money, few brains and boundless energy, we began digging in a mood of high adventure. It was well that we did, for we had just that.

Digging through the topsoil was child's play, but when we struck the hard clay subsoil things got rough. It was a labor of love but it was still labor, and the work began going more slowly. Spring rains caused cave-ins, making it necessary to haul more buckets of earth to the surface. But the thing that upset us the most, and the most frequently, were the encounters we had with gas pockets. We know now what we didn't know then, that our land is probably over a large natural gas reservoir. We didn't pay too much attention to the little pockets but one day we struck a big one that scared the bejabbers out of both of us. We got out of the hole so fast we almost knocked each other over going up the ladder. When things subsided we continued the work cautiously and all went well.

Finally we did strike a good seepage of water at around 22 feet, and Carl cased the well and put it on a pump. Of course this is surface water and we use it for nothing but irrigation, but it still comes in mighty handy. Though we now have ample supplies of water and rationing is a thing of the past the rates have increased, so we enjoy having this good supply of our own for supplemental use.

Of course our Pecan trees get their full share and respond well to it during the growing season, for lack of enough moisture in late spring or early summer results in the production of small nuts. And insufficient water in August and September results in poorly filled nuts.

Water is important for other reasons. Trees have neither teeth nor digestive systems for breaking down organic food. They only have the ability to absorb the nutrient elements dissolved in water. They, like all other plants, live on a liquid diet. Their food elements must be transported up the stem and into the leaves in liquid form. When this occurs, small amounts of simple chemicals and large amounts of water are broken down and combine with the carbon from the air.

The end products of this combination are the starches and sugars, the energy fuels found in the seeds, or the nuts if you prefer. Lack of water can be a limiting factor, for without enough of it growth is impossible.

Remember, too, that Pecan and other nut trees on a homesite are in competition with lawn grasses for available moisture, and normal lawn watering is not adequate for them. Once a month, during the spring and fall and every two to three weeks during the summer, let a hose run for several hours under the trees. If you keep your trees well mulched, as suggested in a previous chapter, the watering will be even more effective and moisture conserved over a longer period of time.

On the other hand remember that water can be just as harmful if present in excess. A young tree standing in a completely saturated soil also can wilt and die. Also plant roots can absorb moisture only if air also is present in the soil. Newly-planted trees often fail because the soil is water-logged — you might say they are "killed with kindness" — because this is a mistake often made by the inexperienced.

This is understandable, because one is constantly told to be sure to keep the tree well watered. With good drainage this may do little harm, but if the tree is planted in a clay hardpan the hole simply holds the water like a basin, the roots become starved for air and the tree dies. So water young trees but do not overwater. The essentials of pruning have been outlined previously, but it bears repeating that Pecans, unlike fruit trees, do not require annual pruning to remain productive. And there is no messy fruit drop to be crushed underfoot and draw flies and other insects. Nut falls are clean and unobtrusive. Pecans are fine trees for *front* yards.

Training and shaping the tree must be done during the first four to five years after planting. A limited amount of corrective pruning always is necessary, of course, to remove limbs which become too low, overcrowded, diseased or damaged by winds, ice, snow or heavy crops.

Though sometimes needed in older groves, the rejuvenation of large Pecan trees by topping or severe de-horning is not generally a practice most homeowners need to follow. Severe pruning of large limbs destroys the natural shape of the tree — one of its best features — and sometimes it permits invasion of insects and diseases. It also eliminates fruiting for two to three years.

Commercial producers use various forms of pruning to keep their trees producing high quality nuts, and aren't greatly concerned about the beauty of the trees. Some varieties respond favorably to a light, annual pruning while others do not. If the homeowner feels that he wants the height and width of his trees reduced, he should avoid pruning of limbs larger than three to four inches in diameter. Cuts of larger diameter rarely heal properly and permit rot organisms to enter and become established. It is important that branches be cut properly, so wounds will callus rapidly, and always to treat any large cut with tree wound dressing.

INSECTS AND DISEASES

During the life of his Pecan trees a homeowner may be faced with insect and disease problems similar to those of the orchard or grove owner, but most can be prevented or controlled by proper pesticide use. The major insects are the Pecan nut

Pecan Weevil causes immature, soft shell nuts to drop, eats kernels of hard shell nuts causes shucks to stick to shells.

casebearer, Hickory shuckworm, Pecan weevils, aphids, Pecan phylloxera and webworms. Others sometimes encountered are mites, Walnut caterpillars, scales, sawfly, May beetles and Pecan catocalas.

Sprays for Pecan nut casebearers usually are applied in May, the exact timing varying from year to year depending on the weather. Question your County Agent for the exact time for treating. Controls for Hickory shuckworms and Pecan weevil (if present) are applied during August and early September. Aphids usually appear from May through October and will need treatment when honeydew appears on the leaves. Pecan phylloxera galls appear just after leaves emerge in the spring. Spraying with a dormant oil will help, and additional insecticide spraying about the time the leaves are one-third grown will reduce the amount of damage. Once the galls are formed, however, no insecticides are effective.

The most serious disease of the Pecan tree throughout most of its growing range is scab, caused by a fungus that damages developing nuts and foliage, particularly in the spring. If this appears, call your County Agent and follow his directions as to the best insecticide to use in your area.

Because of the high cost of adequate spray equipment and the small number of trees, it may be too expensive to control insects and diseases for nut production in yard trees. But if nut production *is* the primary objective, spray equipment necessary for proper coverage may be rented or purchased. Coverage is extremely important, though control of some diseases and insects may be obtained by using a garden hose-type sprayer, with a stepladder to gain additional height. And to reduce drift be sure to apply pesticides when weather conditions are suitable. In other words choose a still day, or when only a very light wind is blowing. Often the time of day is important, and in my area I find that early morning is often a good time for spraying.

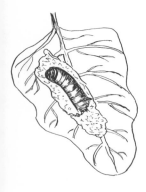

The Casebearer larva makes holes in buds. and leaves.

A good dormant oil spray for phylloxera (galls) may be made of one pint of very light oil (10 weight) mixed with two cups soap or detergent. Mix thoroughly and then add four gallons of water. Spray the entire tree at one time, and be sure to do this in late winter before any leaf buds begin to open. This is when insects that hatch from eggs laid the previous fall can be most readily killed. Now the shells of the eggs and the protective covering of hibernating scales are softer and more porous and the dormant spray can penetrate, making a tight, continuous film over them. It literally suffocates the organisms.

Always do your spraying before leaves appear, because the oil would also form a similar injurious film over them and cause them to drop. It is impossible to give exact dates for a spray schedule in all sections of the country, but here is one that can be followed in most Southern states. Consult your County Agent for best times in your area.

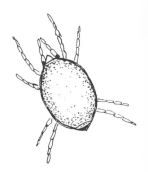

Mites cause leaves to turn a uniform reddish brown.

Time	Pest	Chemicals
Prepollination	Scab	Fungicide and zinc
May	Scab	Fungicide, insecticide and zinc
May to October	Aphids, mites and leaf-feeding caterpillars	Insecticide
August 15	Hickory shuck-worm, scab	Insecticide and fungicide
September 1	Pecan weevil, Hickory shuckworm	Insecticide
September 15	Pecan weevil, Hickory shuck-worm	Insecticide

The insecticides most often used by homeowners to control Pecan insects are Malathion and Sevin, which will mix with zinc sulfate and fungicides. Use the chemicals according to directions given on the labels, and always wash hands and face thoroughly and put on clean clothing after using sprays of any type. If any spraying material is left over, store in a safe place (being sure to label), or dispose of the sprayer contents.

The sprays and spraying schedule just given should be followed by the homeowner interested in producing quality nuts. If maintaining an attractive landscape tree is the primary consideration, a minimum of one or two sprays in April-May for rosette and scab should be applied. In addition, one or more sprays should be used as necessary during the summer and early fall to minimize leaf damage and premature defoliation caused by aphids, mites and leaf-feeding caterpillars.

HARVESTING PECANS

This is what we really have been waiting for, and it is truly a glorious time of year. Spring has its beauties but autumn brings the harvest, and to my way of thinking it can be just as lovely.

Some of the happiest times I remember are the family picnics we used to have at Pecan picking time. We would all go to an early service at the church, then I would pack a lunch, and my husband and I with our children would drive to the Pecan orchard. In the early part of the season pickers would be paid according to the poundage, and the orchard would keep the Pecans. Some orchards provided mechanical means of shaking the trees to hasten the fall, but high winds usually made the fall pretty good anyhow. Later in the season, when most of the nuts had been gathered, the orchard would move to picking on a different basis called "on the halves." A hundred pounds of nuts, for instance, would be divided equally between the picker and the orchard. We called this "scrapping," and in many years a diligent picker could do very well for himself.

We always picked "as a family," putting all the nuts gathered into one or several sacks, stopping at noon to rest and have our picnic lunch, and then continuing on in the afternoon. When we were tired and ready to go home we would drag our pecans to the weighing shack and receive our share.

We divided this share again equally among the four of us, even the littlest child receiving the same amount. Carl and I always kept ours for home use but the children sold theirs if they wished, netting a modest amount to be used for Christmas spending money.

Usually our own trees would produce a good crop too, and this would be added to the family share when "cracking time" began. This always took place as soon as possible after picking, and it still does. I am of the opinion that Pecans should be shelled right after gathering. You will have less shattering of shells and more whole halves. The nuts are easy to get out of the shells, are of prime flavor and can be stored at their very best. The Dynamic Nutcracker, (L.H. Powell, 8647 Wingate, Dallas, Texas 75209) an electric nutcracker for home use, is by far the best machine I have ever used for cracking Pecans. There is no adjusting for size of nut, and it is fast and efficient. It will also crack other thin-shelled nuts just as easily. A plexiglass shield prevents shells from scattering. Pecans come out almost 100 percent in whole halves. After cracking I always freeze my Pecans in moisture-proof containers, and their keeping qualities are excellent.

I realize that this method is not always possible for those who live in other areas, so here are some hints on how to shell Pecans if the nuts are dry. The percentage of whole kernels may be increased by soaking the nuts in water overnight (10 hours). Or boiling water may be poured over the nuts, allowing them to soak 15 to 30 minutes, depending upon the thickness of the shell.

Either treatment tends to make the kernels more pliable, and they will hold together better during the shelling operation, which is best done as soon as the Pecans are dry. Two pounds will yield about one pound (four cups) of shelled nutmeats.

PECANS ADD FLAVOR TO FOOD

Pecans may be used in many ways to give a distinctive and delicious flavor to foods. They are unexcelled for use in candy, ice cream, pastries or for eating roasted and salted. Pecans add richness and flavor to stuffing for poultry, to croquettes, creamed chicken, fish and salads, and they are well adapted for use in biscuits, muffins and waffles, as well as other types of bread, in cakes, cookies and other desserts. They are excellent substitutes in recipes calling for other kinds of nut meats.

This is the way the famous Louisiana praline came to be invented. It actually was originated near Orleans, France in the reign of Louis XV by Jean Dulac, the chef who had charge of the kitchen of Gabrial De Choiseul, the Duc de Praslin. The Duc, a very important man in charge of marine and foreign affairs, was especially fond of candies, and liked to share them with his lady friends.

One day the Duc, running out of his favorite bonbons, sent his valet flying to the kitchen where the following recipe was quickly put together using the ingredients that happened to be on hand:

2 cups sugar,   cherry flavoring
    brown   3 cups Almonds
1 teaspoon soda   2 tablespoons butter
1 cup buttermilk
pinch salt

Boil the first four ingredients three minutes. Add Almonds and butter. Cook until it forms a very soft ball in cold water. Remove from fire and let set one or two minutes. Beat until thick and creamy. Drop by spoonfuls on waxed paper (originally a marble slab was used). (Note: cook in a rather large vessel as soda causes mixture to foam up.) Stir all the time candy is cooking to keep from scorching.

The hastily prepared dainties were such a success that the Duc gave them his name of "Praslin" which gradually was changed to the name "Praline", the French pronunciation. "Praslin".

One story has it that fleeing nobility brought the recipe to New Orleans at the time of the French Revolution, another that it was brought to the New World by the Ursuline Nuns. Probably both are true. Almonds in Louisiana were scarce or entirely unobtainable, so Pecans were substituted, and the cherry flavoring, called for in the original recipe, was left out for the same reason.

The praline has survived flood, war, plague, and politics. Its popularity has never waned, and the only change in nearly two hundred years has been the method by which it is sold. It was once made and sold exclusively by Negro women on the streets of the city. Now it is sold behind the counters of dozens of French Quarter shops.

Here is a more modern delicacy which my family enjoys:

PECAN RECIPES

pecan praline

Mix and combine:
1 cup sugar
½ teaspoon salt
3 teaspoon cinnamon
3 teaspoons cinnamon
6 tablespoons milk
Cook without stirring to soft ball stage, 240° F. for five minutes.
Add ½ teaspoon vanilla
3 cups roasted Pecans
Stir until stiff and pour on waxed paper.

Roasted Pecans, good in themselves, may be either dry-roasted or have butter, margarine or oil added. Place Pecan halves in pan and turn over to low heat. Stir occasionally, testing from time to time for crispness. Do not let them get too brown, as flavor will be impaired. Salt may be added if Pecans are to be used as dry-roasted nuts.

Other favorites which everyone enjoys are:

pecan pie

Prepare a plain pastry and line 9 inch pie pan.
3 eggs
½ cup sugar
1 cup dark corn syrup
⅛ teaspoon salt
1 teaspoon vanilla
2 tablespoons melted butter
    or margarine
1 cup Pecan meats
Beat eggs slightly. Add sugar, syrup, salt, vanilla and butter. Place the Pecans in the bottom of the pastry-lined pan. Add the filling. Bake at 400° F. for 10 minutes, then reduce heat to 350° F. and bake until mixture sets (30 to 35 minutes). The nuts will rise to the top and form a crusted layer.

pecan waffles

2 cups sifted all-purpose flour
3 teaspoons baking powder
¼ teaspoon salt
¾ cup chopped Pecans
2 eggs separated
6 tablespoons shortening, melted
Sift together dry ingredients, and add Pecans. Beat egg yolks until light, combine with milk and melted shortening and add to dry ingredients, mixing until just smooth. Beat egg whites until stiff and fold into batter. Bake in hot, well-oiled waffle iron. Yields 6-9 waffles.

plum-pecan cake

2 cups *self-rising* flour
2 cups sugar
1 teaspoon cinnamon
1 teaspoon cloves
¼ teaspoon nutmeg
1 teaspoon salt
3 eggs
1 cup corn oil
2 jars plum baby food
    (small)
1 cup Pecans, chopped
    or run through on coarse
    grind)
Sift dry ingredients together twice. Add well-beaten eggs, corn oil, plum baby food and Pecans. Mix well and pour into a well-greased and lightly floured tube pan and bake in a preheated 350° F. oven for one hour. Allow to set for 15 minutes before removing from pan. Serve uniced or dribble over it:
2 cups powdered sugar
2 tablespoons melted margarine
Enough lemon juice to mix sugar and margarine to spread well.

pecan cranberry orange quick bread

2 cups all-purpose flour
1 cup sugar
1½ teaspoons baking powder
½ teaspoon soda
1½ teaspoons salt
½ cup corn oil
¾ cup orange juice
1 teaspoon grated orange peel
1 egg, well beaten
1 cup chopped Pecans
1 cup raw cranberries, chopped

Sift dry ingredients twice. Add other ingredients and mix well. Pour into well-oiled loaf pan and bake in moderately slow oven (325° F.) for one hour until crust is golden brown. Allow to set on wire rack 10 minutes. Remove from pan. Cool. Store overnight for easy slicing. Thin slices buttered make delicious tea sandwiches.

pecan brownies

2 eggs
1 cup sugar
½ cup sifted flour
6 tablespoons cocoa
¼ teaspoon salt
1 teaspoon baking powder
½ cup butter (or margarine)
    melted
1 teaspoon vanilla
1 cup Pecans

Beat eggs. Add sugar and sifted dry ingredients. Stir in butter, vanilla and Pecans. Spread in shallow oiled 8-inch square pan. Bake in 350° F. oven, 20 to 30 minutes. Cool slightly. Cut into 1 x 2-inch bars or 2-inch squares.

banana nut loaf

Mix together:
2/3 cup sugar
1/3 cup shortening
2 eggs
3 tablespoons sour milk
1 cup mashed bananas
½ teaspoon soda
½ cup chopped Pecans
1 teaspoon salt
Sift together and stir in:
2 cups flour
1 teaspoon baking powder
Pour into well-oiled 9 x 5 x 3-inch loaf pan. Let stand 20 minutes before baking. Bake loaf until it tests done, about 50 to 60 minutes, at 350° F.

cinnamon nut rolls

2 cups lukewarm milk
½ cup sugar
2 teaspoons salt
2 eggs
7 to 7½ cups sifted flour
2 cakes compressed yeast
½ cup soft shortening
½ cup chopped Pecans
Roll dough into oblong 9 x 8-inches. Spread with 2 tablespoons softened butter (or margarine) and sprinkle with ½ cup sugar, 2 teaspoons cinnamon, ¼ teaspoon nutmeg, ½ cup chopped Pecans. Roll up together. Cut roll into 1-inch slices. Place a little apart in oiled 13 x 9-inch pan or 18 muffin cups. Cover and let rise until double in bulk, 35 to 50 minutes. Bake in 375° F. oven 20 to 25 minutes.

spiced (deviled) pecans

2 tablespoons margarine
1 tablespoon Worcestershire sauce
¼ teaspoon garlic powder (optional)
1 cup Pecan halves
Salt and cayenne pepper
    to taste

Heat oven to 350° F. Place margarine in a skillet. Add the sauce and blend while margarine melts. Add Pecans, garlic powder, salt and cayenne. Stir and toss until nuts are coated. Roast in oven 20 minutes, stirring occasionally. Drain on absorbent paper and sprinkle with additional salt if desired. (Note: Be sure to roast at low heat and do not let nuts get too brown.)

pecan brittle

2 cups sugar
¼ teaspoon salt
¼ teaspoon soda
1 teaspoon vanilla
2 cups chopped
    Pecans

Heat the sugar gradually in iron skillet over low heat. Stir constantly with the bowl of a spoon until completely melted and golden brown in color. Remove from heat and quickly add salt, soda and vanilla, stirring just enough to mix. Pour the syrup over a layer of Pecans in a buttered pan. As soon as it can be handled, pull and stretch it out into a thin sheet. When cold break into irregular pieces.

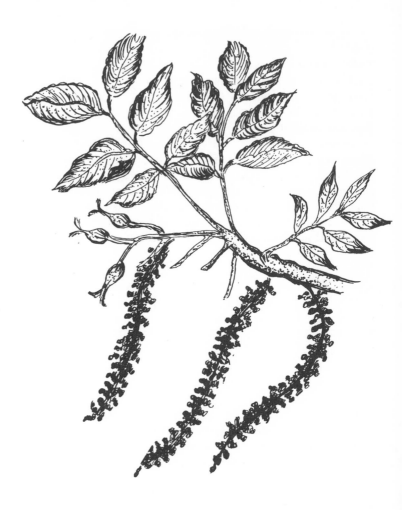

5

BLACK WALNUT BUTTERNUT & HEARTNUT

The food value of Black Walnuts is amazing, in calories per pound outdistancing beefsteak more than three times! Moreover, they contain 27.6 percent protein, so their value as a diet addition is readily apparent. And the Black Walnut retains its flavor after cooking.

Perhaps early man sensed these advantages instinctively, for there is evidence the Walnut was enjoyed by primitive inhabitants of the Middle West where it flourishes today. Here Black Walnut shells, crudely carved in the form of birds and pierced to serve as earrings, have been discovered among the bones and pottery fragments of the Mound Builders of Ohio and Indiana.

My first experience with Black Walnuts occurred a number of years ago when it became necessary to clear some of the timber on a small ranch property. Black Walnuts grow wild here in Oklahoma and, as luck would have it, there were a number of these trees on the land, as well as Pecans and Hickories. To make room for a small house a few of them had to be felled.

We kept part of the lumber, and when it was well cured my

husband made some of it into very lovely pieces of furniture. I prize this now more than ever, for its beauty has increased through the years and they are of *solid* walnut, not veneer. The lumber we did not keep was sold for a good price even in those days and, of course, would bring far more now.

The property had been neglected for years when it came into my possession, and it was necessary to clear out underbrush, as well as a few trees which were crowding the others. Of course I kept every nut tree possible, but a few had to go, so that the remaining ones would have room. Nut trees, like fruit trees, should have full exposure to the sun if they are to produce at their best.

I well remember the first year after this work, how disappointed I was that my Black Walnuts did not bear well. What was wrong? Actually nothing, and the following year the trees came through with a bumper crop. I had lots to learn.

Walnuts vary in their bearing habits. Though some trees yield heavily every year (as my *Thomas* variety Black Walnut does), most native trees growing in the wild furnish a crop in two and three-year cycles. As things turned out mine were the type that bore every other year — bushels one year but very few nuts the next. Even so, that big crop is well worth waiting for, since the established trees require virtually no care. We keep the land mowed so there is no weed or brush problem. Certain grasses grow well under Black Walnut trees, St. Augustine in southern regions and bluegrass in the North.

The only pruning required is the occasional removal of sprouts from the trunks. We have found that if we do this in the fall, when they are under an inch or so in diameter, they are easily trimmed with pruning shears.

The nuts from my native trees are a good size, averaging from an inch to an inch-and-a-quarter each. So one day I decided to plant some of them on our town property.

I chose a spot on the northwest corner hoping that when the tree grew it might be seen and admired from several directions. The Black Walnut *(Juglans nigra)* is far too beautiful to put behind the house. The name *Juglans,* by the way, is said to be derived from the Latin *Jovis glans* or "Jupiter's Acorn."

Knowing very little about nut culture I simply dug a hole a few inches deep, put in two or three of the largest Walnuts and hoped for the best. Maybe I was just lucky. Maybe by accident I did the right thing.

Hidden in the ground that winter, the shells soaked up

moisture while the frost cracked them — nature's way of getting things ready. Thus, when spring approached, the young plants were encouraged to strike out and take root, which they made haste to do.

Now I know that nurserymen get the same results by laying the Walnuts in a bed of sand or gravel, one layer above another, and letting the rain and cold do the rest. This "stratification" differs somewhat from Pecans and here is how it should be done if you want to plant Black Walnut seeds (nuts) in quantity.

STRATIFICATION

Stratification is the method of carrying seeds through the period from the time they are ripe until they are ready to germinate. It provides a means of doing this with minimum trouble and space.

Seeds of certain trees will not germinate soon after they ripen, yet will lose their viability if they are allowed to dry. The Black Walnut is one of these, differing from the Pecan which does not fall into dormancy.

Black Walnut seeds need a storage period of several months at low termperatures in a moist, dark place before they are ready to grow. In nature such conditions are provided for by the seeds falling to the ground in the autumn or early winter where they are soon covered by forest debris, assuring darkness and preventing drying. When I planted the nuts in my yard, soon after they were harvested, these conditions were met, and the winter months provided the necessary low temperatures.

Most gardeners, however, find it more convenient to stratify such seeds rather than sowing them immediately. Stratification provides the necessary conditions without the seeds taking up much space, and they require far less attention than if they were planted immediately after they were gathered.

Stratification is accomplished by mixing the seeds with sand or sand and peat moss that is just moist. They are then stored where they will remain moist and cool.

A convenient way is to place layers of sand, or sand and peat moss, alternately with layers of seeds in wooden boxes. The boxes are then buried outdoors about six inches deep in a shaded area where the soil is well drained. Surrounding the boxes with wire netting before burial is a wise precaution to foil rodents which might dig up the seeds. If they freeze it won't hurt them.

If you wish to stratify only a few seeds, another way is to place a dozen or so nuts in a jar of moist sand, or sand and peat moss, and place them in the refrigerator.

PLANTING

Whatever storage method you choose to use, the seeds should be removed from the mixing medium to be sown in the regular way in pots, flats, coldframes or out of doors when conditions are right for them to germinate.

Well-drained, light, loamy soil is best. If seeds can be sown in places where the trees are to grow, this is a definite advantage, for root injury at transplanting time may cause a serious check in growth. Young plants that were sown as seed in a nursery bed should be lifted at the end of the first year and the roots carefully trimmed; they then should be replanted. Every second year the trees should be transplanted until they can be planted in permanent places.

Black Walnut trees grow best in rich, loose soils of limestone origin that are at least four feet deep. Since the trees develop deep taproots, the subsoil should be easy for the roots to penetrate.

The soil must be well-drained and not strongly acid. The trees will not grow well in bottomland where the soil often is saturated. They will not grow well or produce large crops on eroded hillsides or other land that will not grow good corn crops. Reliable indicators of suitable land for growing Walnuts is the presence of good stands of white oak and tulip-poplar.

Black Walnut trees may be transplanted either in autumn or spring, but early spring is considered best in most areas, since then new roots will grow quickly to replace those lost in transplanting. In the South young trees may be planted either in fall or winter, but fall trees planted north of the Ohio and Potomac Rivers will not have time to grow new roots before the ground freezes, and they may die.

SPACING

Black Walnuts, as native to much of the United States east of the Great Plains, will produce nut crops on a wide variety of sites and soil types within their natural range. The trees also can be grown for shade and ornamental purposes for a few hundred miles outside of their natural range, but may not produce nuts there.

The Black Walnut at maturity is a very large tree, attaining as much as 150 feet, and it is also a long-lived tree. For this reason trees planted either for ornamental use or nut production should be spaced at least 60 feet apart to give the branches and roots adequate space in which to spread out.

SETTING TREES

Examine your trees when they are received and cut off any broken or ragged roots, using a slanting cut. If you cannot plant immediately, keep the trees (especially the roots) moist, and plant as soon as possible.

For trees up to seven feet tall, dig a hole two feet deep and three feet wide. Place the tree at the same depth in the hole as it stood in the nursery row and spread the roots out well. As with the Pecan, the taproot must be buried vertical all the way. Curling it around a little just won't get the job done right, so play fair both with the tree and yourself.

Refill the hole with topsoil about half way, working it well in around the roots. Tamp the soil with your foot or a blunt stick. Continue filling and repeat the procedure, tamping the soil down until the ground is firm. Then form a basin around the edge of the hole with extra soil and soak the soil immediately. Repeat this a time or two as the water soaks in and then do not water again until necessary (see "other requirements" below).

Plant one tree at a time and finish the whole job before starting on another one. Keep the roots of the others covered in damp burlap or in a pail of water to prevent drying by sun and wind.

FERTILIZER REQUIREMENTS

Black Walnut trees need large amounts of nitrogen and

potassium and small amounts of phosphorus for best growth and nut production. Even if you are lucky enough, as I was, to inherit a few native trees, you will find that nut production can be improved in both quantity and quality by a good feeding program.

Do not mix any fertilizer in the soil, however, when planting trees, nor is it advisable to use any during the first spring, because of the danger of injuring roots. Well-decomposed compost or leaf mold may be mixed with the soil at planting time, but fresh manure should never be used.

After the first year mixed fertilizers, applied annually, will benefit both young trees and older ones. Spread it evenly under the tree branches when the buds begin to swell in early spring. To fertilize yard trees apply a little more under the tree branches than you normally would use on your lawn.

Trees grown near barns or in stock or poultry yards, perhaps to provide shade, benefit from the natural addition of manures and usually flourish. For trees that do not have this benefit you can spread and work lightly into the soil around the trees a mixture of balanced minerals and fertilizers. These may be equal parts of cottonseed meal or blood meal, phosphate rock or bone meal, wood ash, granite dust or greensand and dolomitic limestone. Water the areas well and, if possible, spread a good leaf mulch around the trees to conserve moisture.

LIME REQUIREMENTS

Strongly acid soils often keep important nutrients unavailable to Black Walnut trees. If your soil is quite acid (again to be determined by a soil test), apply enough lime to raise the pH to 6 or 6.5.

pH simply means the active acidity or alkalinity of anything, expressed in units, and in horticultural science it indicates the condition of the soil. Many plants will thrive only when the pH value of the soil closely approximates the optimum for their particular kind. In other words, if the soil isn't naturally to the liking of the tree or plants, you've got to change the soil condition to have success.

But liming, if it is found necessary, should be approached with caution. Overliming makes the zinc in the soil unavailable to the tree. As with the Pecan this is an element necessary to the

Black Walnut.

Soils east of the Mississippi River sometimes are deficient in magnesium, but crushed dolomitic limestone — which contains magnesium oxide — will correct this and reduce the acidity of your soil, too. Your County Agent can arrange to test the soil for its acidity and an analysis of its nutrient needs. Or you may send a soil sample to your State Agricultural Experiment Station or a private laboratory for analysis.

OTHER REQUIREMENTS

Black Walnut trees often need to be watered and have other care to grow well and produce large nut crops. Because of their deep taproots, however, the trees are drought resistant. Keep an area about four feet in diameter around each tree cleared of weeds and grasses that would compete for water and nutrients or, do as I do, and mulch heavily. If for the sake of appearance you do not wish to mulch a yard tree at least be sure to water it regularly while it is young, because of competition with grass for moisture. A good soaking weekly, unless there is natural rainfall, probably is a good general rule.

The part of your tree that is below the graft (if you have grafted trees) may produce suckers. Prune these off at the trunk while small or they may crowd out the shoot that is growing from the variety scion.

On a ranch or homestead, do not allow livestock to graze around your young trees. When they are 15 years old, however, they can be inter-seeded with grasses and legumes, and animals turned in to pasture will not damage them.

As with other newly-planted trees, wrapping the trunk to prevent sunscald and insect invasion is always a wise precaution. If your section is very windy it also is well to stake the tree for the first year or two until it has had time to become established.

PRUNING

Pruning is necessary when a tree is young to encourage a single leading shoot, to check undue growth of side branches and to keep the lower part of the trunk clear. Be sure to do any necessary pruning between June and the latter part of December. If Black Walnut trees, whether large or small, are pruned during late winter and spring, they tend to "bleed" profusely, and it is difficult to check.

GRAFTING BLACK WALNUTS

The Black Walnuts I planted from "wild" seed grew very well, and the appearance of the little trees with their bright, lustrous, yellow-green leaves was a delight. All were so pretty, dancing in the breeze, that it was hard to make a choice, but I knew I must, for three definitely was "a crowd." In the fall of the first year I pulled two of my seedlings, leaving the largest to grow without competition for the nutrients in the soil.

In early winter, after the tree had lost its leaves, I dug in some thoroughly decomposed compost, being careful neither to get too near the tree nor to go too deep. After this I mulched it with leaves.

Since Black Walnut trees grow wild in many places in Oklahoma, I wasn't particularly worried about the tree surviving that first winter. I was far more interested in helping it make good growth. I wanted things to be ready the following year when it began to grow again and put out leaves, and I felt that plenty of organic matter in the soil would encourage this.

This program was followed for the next few years and my tree continued to show satisfactory progress. Then the time had come for the next step. Carl, my husband, who is a graduate of New York State Agricultural College, showed me how to whip graft the tree, using *Thomas* scions. Bark grafting or patch budding (see Chapter III), of course, may also be used to top work Black Walnut trees. Carl chose whip grafting scions since they grow well from rooted stock. Such scions are usually taken from dormant wood between late fall and early spring and must have one or more buds. And he chose *Thomas* scions for their dependability. Unlike our native trees they bear a full crop of nuts every year — at least here in our area they have never failed to do so. Note also that the Black Walnut is also desirable root stock for Persian (English) and Siebold Walnuts, Heartnuts and Butternuts.

The graft took well, and the year the tree first blossomed we watched it eagerly. Would it or wouldn't it bear nuts? Walnuts

Whip or tongue graft

are monoecious, (the male and female blossoms separate on the same tree).

Many seedling trees are persistently unfruitful because the male and female flowers do not open at the same time. To overcome this problem, provision for cross-pollination usually is made by growing two or three trees reasonably near each other. As there are other Black Walnut trees in our immediate neighborhood we were in luck in this respect.

The first year that our little tree produced we watched the nuts grow all summer, and by fall it was proudly displaying about two dozen greenish, ball-shaped hulls. These turned yellow and then brown after they dropped from the tree. These thick, pulpy and bitter hulls really are a protective covering. They frustrate the squirrels and keep them from gnawing into the nut until it is dry and brittle.

THE HARVEST

Black Walnuts do not open their husks in regular segments as do the Hickories (including Pecans), and sometimes we spread them on the roof of a low building so they can dry while the nuts are seasoning.

There are a number of ways for handling Black Walnuts in order to remove them from the husks, and you can take your choice. The hulls do stain the fingers if handling becomes necessary, but this can be avoided by wearing a pair of rubber household gloves. This stain was used in an older day for dyeing cloth, and people sometimes stained their faces and hands with Walnut juice as a disguise.

We had some friends who devised a hulling method all their own. They put on heavy shoes and "stomped" the nuts with a sliding motion of the foot, thus rolling them out of their hulls. The nuts then were placed in successive buckets of water and agitated until practically all of the spongy substance was removed. Then they were spread out to dry.

We think an easier way is to place the nuts on the driveway and drive the pickup truck over them slowly, forward and then back several times. If two people work at this and the second member of the team keeps shoveling the nuts (a square shovel is handy for his) under the wheels, the work goes faster. The abrasive action of the tires usually is sufficient.

But there is still another way of using the rear wheel of an automobile as an effective hull remover. Fit one of the rear wheels with a tire chain and jack up the rear with just enough room beneath the tire for the nuts to pass. The chain will remove the hulls as the nuts are forced through a trough below the slowly turning wheel.

After the hulls are off, the nuts should be thoroughly washed and spread out to dry away from direct sunlight for two or three weeks. The nuts then can be stored in a cool, dry place until needed. Nuts that float in water usually contain dry kernels and may be discarded.

Lightly-colored Walnut kernels have a milder flavor than dark ones. If you prefer light kernels, harvest the nuts as soon as they drop from the trees in the autumn. Leaving them on the ground until the hulls partially decompose causes the kernels to discolor.

It is difficult to extract kernels in large pieces from most varieties of Black Walnuts because of the thick shell and the convolutions of the kernel. The nuts can be tempered by soaking them in water for an hour or two, then keeping them moist overnight in a closed container. The kernels absorb enough moisture to become slightly tough temporarily, yet remain loose in the shell.

The shells of many Walnuts are thick and hard, though the grafted varieties have somewhat thinner shells as well as larger kernels and are therefore easier to crack, yet care is necessary to avoid breaking the meats. Many mechanical devices are used to crack Pecans but, so far as I know there is no commercial machine in use for Walnuts. There are, however, specially-designed small hand crackers which will do the work much better than a hammer. A pound of Walnuts will yield about a third of a pound of shelled nutmeats or approximately one cup. The nuts are sweet and very rich in oil, so rich in fact that a few at a time eaten out of hand or added to other foods are usually satisfying.

There is a good market for Black Walnuts. Candy makers, bakers of bread and cake and even ice cream manufacturers buy them in quantity. Unlike many other nuts, Black Walnuts retain their flavor when cooked.

BLACK WALNUT VARIETIES

Several improved, grafted varieties of Black Walnut trees are available, and their nuts are far superior to those of native trees grown from seed. Three of the most widely planted improved types are *Thomas, Ohio* and *Myers*. They start bearing nuts the second or third year after they are planted, while native trees do not start bearing until about ten years old.

At five or six years of age *Thomas* and *Ohio* each produce about one-fourth of a bushel of nuts, and *Myers* produces about one-eighth of a bushel. At 15 to 20 years *Thomas* and *Ohio* produce about two bushels of nuts, *Myers* produces about one bushel, and native trees grown from seedlings about one-fourth of a bushel. Nuts produced by native trees usually have thick and heavy shells, while *Thomas* and *Ohio* nuts have thinner shells, and *Myers* nuts have the thinnest of all. Disease resistance varies with the varieties — see under "Walnut Problems."

In addition to the varieties mentioned, many nurseries now have developed superior strains of their own. The Burgess Seed and Plant Company, for instance, by special breeding has produced a strain that is a proven, dependable year-after-year bearer of extra large crops, and the plump meats crack out of the shells easily. Stark Bros. have developed the *Boellner* strain, called the *Stark Kwik-Krop* Black Walnut, which bears young and heavily, usually within two years after planting. The nuts are large, slightly pointed, and have relatively thin shells for easy cracking.

Many nurseries still offer the grafted *Thomas* Walnut, a general favorite. The kernels are large and of good flavor, bringing a good price on the market because most of the meats can be gotten out in halves and quarters. My *Thomas* Walnut is a consistent bearer and produces a crop every year.

Of course grafted trees are higher in price. So if you live outside the area where Black Walnuts can be expected to bear good crops, you may wish to purchase less expensive trees for landscape use or windbreaks. These also are available, or you can grow your own.

BLACK WALNUT TREES

Native trees, either grown from seed or purchased, may be

just what you want, if you have adequate acreage, to plant for timber stands. It has been said that "He who plants a tree loves others besides himself," and indeed a stand of Walnut timber could be a greater inheritance to leave a son or daughter than stocks or bonds!

In the forests of long ago in the basin of the Ohio and Wabash rivers, giant Walnut trees 150 feet tall were not uncommon, holding their majestic heads far above the tops of the oaks and maples. Unfortunately they were slaughtered, rolled together and burned by the early pioneers who were intent upon clearing the land for agriculture.

Unhappily the growing of young trees to replace those destroyed has never been undertaken extensively, but as we become more aware of this need there is hope that it will be.

Walnuts especially are so beautiful in full leaf that a tree, even one on the home grounds, is a never ending pleasure. The bark is dark but the tree is never somber, for the foliage is bright and lustrous, graceful and dancing in every breeze. I think Walnuts deserve more use in landscaping and for parks. No tree is more interesting to watch as it grows.

GRAFTED BLACK WALNUTS

(This does not represent a complete list of all varieties)

Variety	Size	Flavor
Sparrow	Medium	Good
Emma K	Medium	Excellent
Elmer Myers	Medium	Excellent
Stambaugh	Large	Good
Drak	Medium	Good
Farrington	Medium	Good
Vandersloot	medium	Good
Baughm No. 25	Medium	Excellent
Boser	Medium	Good
Mintle	Small	Excellent
Stabler	Medium	Good
Victoria	Large	Good
Ohio	Large	Good
Thomas	Medium	Good

BLACK WALNUT PROBLEMS

The most serious diseases of Black Walnut, Walnut anthracnose and bunch disease, attack the tree throughout its natural range.

Walnut anthracnose, or leaf blotch, is a fungus disease that destroys the leaves. It overwinters in fallen leaves, and the first infection by the spores on new leaflets occurs from the middle of May until the middle of June.

Infected leaflets develop many circular, dark-brown spots, ranging from one-sixteenth to five-sixteenths of an inch in diameter, and these often merge to form large dead areas with yellow borders. The infected leaflets usually drop from the trees by late July or early August.

In years of severe infection, the trees may be entirely defoliated, and many of the nuts are empty or contain blackened and shriveled kernels. Badly infected trees grow little, are greatly weakened and are more vulnerable to winter injury.

The disease can be controlled by four applications of a

Cracking	Bearing	No. of Years
Excellent	Prolific	3-5 Years
Excellent	Prolific	3-5 Years
Excellent	Medium	3-5 Years
Very Good	Medium	3-5 Years
Excellent	Prolific	3-5 Years
Very Good	Prolific	3-5 Years
Very Good	Prolific	3-5 Years
Excellent	Medium	3-5 Years
Very Good	Prolific	3-5 Years
Fair	Prolific	3-5 Years
Good	Medium	3-5 Years
Poor	Prolific	3-5 Years
Good	Medium	3-5 Years
Fair	Medium	3-5 Years

fungicide spray each year. Start the treatment when the Walnut fronds approach 12 inches in length, and apply at two week intervals. Don't wait for spots to appear before spraying, or serious damage will have been done. Trees ranging from 15 to 25 feet tall will need five to ten gallons of spray each in each application. Low-lime Bordeaux spray will give good control. For this mix one cup of lime and one-and-a-third cups of copper sulfate with 10 gallons of water.

The *Ohio* variety is resistant to the disease, but in years of severe infection may be defoliated. *Meyers* usually is more resistant than native trees, but less so than *Ohio. Thomas* is the least resistant of the improved varieties.

Bunch disease is caused by a virus that stunts the growth of Black Walnut trees and lowers nut production. The means of spread and of infection are unknown.

Infected trees in mid-summer develop bushy, broomlike shoots on branches and also upright, suckerlike shoots on trunks and main branches. Some shoots die back during late summer and others are killed during the winter. In addition, leaflets narrow, curl and turn yellow.

Preventing healthy trees from becoming infected is the only known method of control. This is done by cutting out and destroying all diseased trees as soon as the bunchy growth is seen.

This disease also attacks Butternut, Heartnut, Pecan and Hickories. If infected, these trees also should be removed.

INSECT PESTS

The insect pests most serious to Black Walnut trees are the Walnut lace bug, curculios, Walnut husk maggot, Walnut caterpillar and fall webworms.

Caution! Many insecticides, including malathion, can be used safely without special protective clothing or devices, provided they are in *dilute* dusts or water sprays. However, most concentrates and oil solutions require special precautions. Exercise care when handling or mixing concentrates to avoid spilling them on the skin, and keep them out of the eyes, nose and mouth. If any is spilled, wash it off the skin and change clothing at once. If any gets in your eyes flush with plenty of water for 15 minutes and get medical attention.

Walnut Lace Bug. This is a fragile, fly-like insect one-fourth of an inch long with lacelike wings, which appears in early summer. Two or three generations may be hatched within a season.

Lace bugs destroy the food-producing ability of the leaves by inserting their mouthparts in the undersides of leaflets and sucking out the juices. This causes the leaves to turn gray and yellow and some may drop prematurely. Since the leaves cannot feed them, the nuts are poorly filled and the tree itself becomes weakened.

The bugs can be controlled by applying an insecticide spray to the foliage when the nuts are pea to marble size. Mix a spray solution of 16 level tablespoons of 25-percent malathion wettable powder with 10 gallons of water. If later generations appear, repeat the spray application. A tree 15 to 25 feet tall may need 5 to 10 gallons of spray in each application.

Curculios. Two species of curculios commonly attack Walnut trees. Both are one-fourth of an inch long, have long, curved snouts and have prominent humps and ridges on their wing covers.

Beginning in June the adults feed on newly-formed nuts and also on new foliage. The females lay their eggs in crescent-shaped punctures in the nuts which will drop before maturing.

To control, collect all prematurely-dropped nuts and burn them immediately to destroy the development of the larvae.

Walnut Husk Maggot. This is a pale yellow fly with brown eyes, stiff brown hairs on the abdomen and transparent wings with dark stripes. The husk maggot hatches from eggs laid in the hulls of maturing Walnuts. The flies appear in early July in the South and in late July in the North. They are in the trees for several weeks before staring to lay eggs. The larva is a white or pale-beige maggot up to a half inch long. The maggots feed in husks of maturing nuts and reduce nuts and reduce the quality of the kernels. Fragments of the hulls cling tenaciously to the shells even after cleaning.

To control, apply malathion when the flies appear. Usually each tree 15 to 25 feet tall will need 5 to 10 gallons of spray in each application.

Walnut Caterpillar. The Walnut caterpillar is the larva of a brown moth that has a wingspan of about two inches. The black caterpillar has white hairs. It distinctively raises both ends of the body when disturbed, feeds in groups on the leaves and causes defoliation. In the North there is a single generation in late

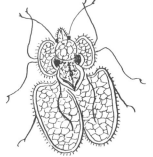

Walnut Lace Bug sucks plant juices.

summer, while in the South there may be generations in early July and in early September. Insecticides applied to other insects usually control this one as well, and special measures generally are not warranted.

Fall Webworm. The fall webworms, the larva of a white moth, reach one inch in length, have black and orange spots and are hairy. Their presence is indicated by distinctive gray webs that enclose branch tips and leaves. There may be early summer and fall generations.

The webworms, which can defoliate Black Walnut trees, feed in groups on leaves inside the webs, enlarging the webs as they need more leaves. They may be controlled by applying insecticide spray to the foliage when the worms are first seen (consult your County Agent as to the best type to use), or the worms can be controlled by pruning off the infested branch tips.

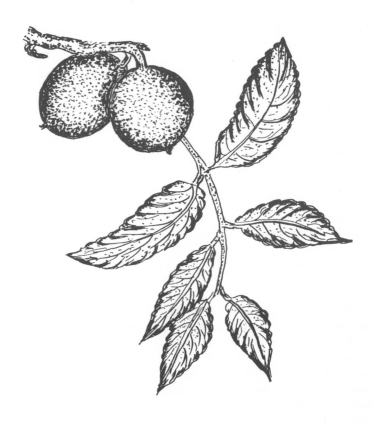

BLACK WALNUT RECIPES

black walnut pie

1 cup brown sugar
2 eggs
½ cup chopped nuts
⅛ teaspoon salt
1½ cups milk, scalded
3 tablespoons cornstarch
1 teaspoon vanilla flavoring
2 tablespoons melted margarine
Combine sugar, margarine, cornstarch and salt. Add milk slowly, stirring constantly. Cook over hot water until thick and smooth. Add slightly beaten egg yoks. Cook 1 minute. Add nuts and flavoring. Fold in stiffly beaten egg whites. Pour into baked pastry shell. Bake in moderate oven (400° F.) until filling is firm.

black walnut cake

2 cups sifted flour (or cake flour)
2 ¾ teaspoons baking powder
¼ teaspoon salt
2/3 cup Crisco
1½ cups sugar
1 teaspoon vanilla
3 eggs
¾ cup milk
1½ cups Black Walnuts, finely chopped
Sift flour, baking powder and salt together. Cream shortening with sugar and vanilla until fluffy. Add beaten egg yolks and beat thoroughly. Add sifted dry ingredients and milk alternately in small amounts, beating well after each addition. Add nuts and fold in stiffly beaten egg whites. Pour into oiled pans and bake in moderate oven (350° F.) 30 minutes. Makes two nine-inch layers.

black walnut meat balls

1½ pounds ground beef
1 cup chopped Walnut meats
2 eggs
½ cup milk
Salt and pepper
2 tablespoons oil
1 can tomato soup
1 cup soft bread crumbs
Combine chopped Walnuts, beef, bread crumbs. Add eggs, milk and seasonings and mix thoroughly. Shape into balls and brown in oil. Add tomato soup and cook slowly for 20 minutes or until meat balls are tender.

Variation: Use onion or mushroom instead of tomato soup.

black walnut cottage pudding

¼ cup margarine
½ cup sugar
1 egg well beaten
¼ teaspoon salt
1 cup milk
2 cups all-purpose flour
3 teaspoons baking powder
½ cup chopped Black Walnuts
½ teaspoon vanilla flavoring
Cream butter with sugar. Add egg. Beat thoroughly. Sift flour, measure and sift with baking powder and salt. Add alternately with milk to first mixture. Add Walnuts and flavoring. Mix thoroughly and pour into shallow, well-oiled baking pan. Bake in moderate oven (375° F.) 30 minutes. Serve with vanilla or hard sauce.

black walnut taffy

2 cups sugar
1 tablespoon margarine
½ cup sweetened condensed milk
½ cup water
½ cup chopped nuts
1 cup molasses
1 teaspoon vanilla flavoring
¼ teaspoon salt

Boil molasses, sugar, salt, milk, water and margarine to hard ball stage (265°-270° F.). Add flavoring. Spread nuts over the bottom of a well-buttered pan. Pour taffy over nuts. Cool. Pull until stiff and creamy. Cut in one-inch pieces.

black walnut cookies

1 cup margarine
1 egg
¼ teaspoon nutmeg
½ cup chopped nuts
1 cup brown sugar
3 cups all purpose flour
¼ teaspoon salt
1 teaspoon vanilla flavoring

Cream margarine and sugar. Add egg and beat well. Sift flour, measure, and sift with salt and nutmeg. Add to creamed mixture. Add nuts. Add flavoring. Mix thoroughly. Form into rolls one-and-a-half inches in diameter. Chill overnight. Cut in thin slices. Place on lightly oiled baking sheet. Bake in hot oven (400° F.) about 10 minutes.

THE BUTTERNUT

This medium-size, spreading tree *(Juglans cinerea)* is known by several names which include White Walnut or Oilnut. The oblong nuts have a rich but delicate flavor and are preferred by many to the stronger-flavored Black Walnut.

A Butternut tree, which reaches 50 to 75 feet in height, is an excellent choice for the home gardener. This is especially true in the northeastern part of the United States, for it is hardier than the Black Walnut and will grow from Maine to Minnesota and south to Arkansas and Georgia.

It is really a shame that the Butternut has not had a better press, for the husked fruit of even the wild Butternut is as large as that of many southern commercial Pecans. The shell of the Pecan is smooth, however, whereas the Butternut shell is very rough, having two major ridges that delineate the suture line, and terminates in a sharp point at one end.

Butternuts, unlike their cousins the Black Walnuts, do not have the intricate internal shell cavities evolved as a protection from rodents, but their rougher shells serve the same purpose. The yield of the shelled nuts is approximately the same as that of Black Walnuts.

In the eastern woods the native Butternut is known by its long, pointed nuts, which have deeply and ruggedly-sculptured shells encased in fuzzy, sticky, green husks that stain the hands of anyone who tries to get at the oily meat before the husks are dry.

Long ago this dark stain was an important dye when homespun cloth was worn by men and boys, and our modern khaki resembles the "butternut jeans" of the backwoods Civil War regiments. The husks and bark also yield a drug that was used for its cathartic properties.

Pickling the soft green nuts was done, also, by housewives in the old days, if nearby woods furnished the raw materials. The recipes were brought to the New World from England, or perhaps from France, by the great-grandmothers of many a woman whose family prizes the delicay today.

To make this preserve it was necessary to test the green nuts with a knitting needle. If it went through them with no difficulty, and the nuts were yet of a good size, they were deemed ready. The nuts were then scalded with boiling water and vigorously rubbed to remove the fuzz. Then the green

Butternuts were pickled whole in spiced vinegar. They provided a delectable relish with meats for the winter table.

Care of the seeds, if you would grow your own, is much the same as for the Black Walnut, in that they are stratified in a bed of sand or gravel, one layer above another, for the cold and rain to do the rest. In spring the nuts are ready for planting. Sometimes when planted careful cracking of the shell helps prepare the nut to sprout.

The preferred method of propagation, however, is to graft Butternuts onto Black Walnut seedlings. This is a tricky operation because of the high pressure and abundant sap flow in the spring, but with care the splice graft usually is successful.

Butternut trees transplant easily, bear young and have the ability to succeed in rather poor soils. There is considerable variation among individual trees both in flavor of the nuts and bearing ability — so be sure to select good stock if grafting is to be practiced.

A Butternut tree does not require as much room as a Black Walnut but it should have ample space in which to grow. It has a short trunk and a low, broad head with downward-drooping horizontal limbs. The bark is light brown and the limbs grayish green. It has one peculiarity — the twigs and leaves all ooze a clammy, waxy, aromatic sap. They also are covered with fine hairs in velvety abundance. The wood of the Butternut is often called "white walnut" and is very beautiful — warm colored, satiny in texture, resistant to warp and enduring. It is a favorite with wood carvers and interior decorators.

Being low and somewhat eccentric in growth, late to leaf out in spring and early to shed its leaves in fall, the Butternut is not considered a good street tree. It also breaks often in areas of high wind, and has numerous insect and fungus enemies. It is usually shorter-lived than its cousin, the Black Walnut in part because it is subject to attack by the Melanconia fungus disease. While not serious for vigorous trees, the fungus is dangerous to those weakened by drought or low fertility.

If this disease becomes apparent (revealed by the small black fruiting pustules of the fungus), the infected limbs should be pruned off some distance below the diseased portion of the branch.

A number of varietal crosses have been made between Butternuts and Siebold Walnuts and some of these are resistant to the Melanconia fungus disease while they retain their leaves much longer than the Butternut.

butternut rolls with cheese

1 lb. grated natural, sharp Cheddar cheese
2 cups sifted, unbleached flour
1 teaspoon salt
¼ pound margarine (1 stick)
½ pound Butternuts, coarsely chopped
Put grated cheese in a mixing bowl and sprinkle with the sifted flour and salt. Cut in the margarine as you would in making pastry. Knead the mixture to a smooth dough. Roll out on a lightly floured board to about ¼-inch thick. Sprinkle as evenly as possible with the Butternuts, pressing them lightly into the dough. Roll as for a jelly roll, wrap in wax paper and chill until firm. Slice into crosswise slices about 1/3-inch thick. Place on teflon cookie sheet and bake at 375° F. until golden brown. Serve at once.

THE HEARTNUT

The Japanese Walnut, *Juglans sieboldiana,* and its variety, *J. sieboldiana cordiformis,* are believed to have been introduced to the United States shortly before 1870 by a nursery in the San Jose valley of California. Actually the Heartnut is just a botanical variety or type of Siebold Walnut. Some authorities believe that the Heartnut is a recessive cross, which occurred long ago, between the original wild Japanese Walnut and the Chinese strain of Persian Walnut, all closely related species.

The Heartnut is a distinctive ornamental tree that grows

about 60 feet high, and has very large leaves and nuts borne in clusters. The trees have a whitish bark which more closely resembles a Persian Walnut than the Butternut or Manchurian Walnut.

The tree grows rapidly, making a low, wide-branched specimen well suited to a larger homestead or ranch-type homesite, but some become quite massive as they age. The foliage is so abundant it gives the tree almost a tropical appearance, while its manner of bearing nuts in long strings is unique.

Heartnuts will withstand low temperatures and may be grown successfully where the Pecan will not thrive. They are grafted in the same manner as Butternuts, and Black Walnut grafting stock may be used. Some Heartnut species may be propagated by layering.

The Japanese Heartnut (Gurney Seed & Nursery Company) grows to a height of about 35 feet and bears young — often as soon as the third year. Its shells are easily cracked. A light tap with a hammer on the suture (the widest dimension) usually will cause most shells to separate, and the sweet, heart-shaped kernels will come out as unbroken halves.

heartnut sausage

1 cup soft white bread crumbs
¼ cup softened margarine
1 cup cooked rice
1½ cups chopped Heartnuts
2 eggs, beaten
¼ teaspoon celery salt
1 tablesppon Worcestershire sauce
½ teaspoon dry, crumbled sage
¼ teaspoon dried thyme
3 tablespoons parsley, fresh or dried
2 tablespoons finely grated onions
½ teaspoon black pepper

Combine all ingredients in a large bowl, tossing together to blend thoroughly. Form into round patties, not too tightly packed. Fry quickly in hot oil on both sides so a light crust is formed. Reduce heat and cook about eight minutes or until done, turning once. Serve with a warm cheese sauce.

6

THE OTHER WALNUTS

Shells of Walnuts have been found in the Swiss Lake dwellings of Neolithic man, dating back to about 7000 B.C. These shells were of the Persian Walnut type, *Juglans regia,* now commonly called "English" (as distinguished from the Black Walnut), because they were first brought to America by the English settlers of Virginia.

Just when the Persian Walnut reached England is open to debate, but many believe that the Romans planted their favorite nut tree during their long occupation of Britain. The English of that period thought of it as a "foreign" tree as evidenced by the word "Walnut," *Wal* deriving from *wealh,* the Old English word for "strange." Another explanation for the name is that they were established in France, then called "Gaul," and the name "Gaul nut," finally was corrupted in English to "Walnut." Linnaeus gave it the specific name "regia" for "royal," quite possibly because of its excellence and the high esteem in which the nut was held, but history also records that Kings made each other presents of these nuts.

English Walnuts were not always the thin shelled, easily

cracked, delicious nut of today. Like native Black Walnuts the nut of the wild tree was small, with a thick, hard shell and a small kernel. The better quality trees and nuts probably were arrived at by a gradual selective process. The best nuts that could be found were planted, and in each succeeding generation the same practice was followed, the pollen being carefully crossed from parent trees, both of proven good stock. Thus, by selection and ever better cross-breeding, the English Walnut (really the Persian) was created with thin shells and fine tasting meat. English Walnuts are frequently grafted on Black Walnut stocks to make the trees hardier, and this practice is followed in California today, where most are grown.

These English Walnuts are of two kinds: the *Santa Barbara* and the *French. Santa Barbaras* are less able to resist heat and cold and require a longer growing season than the *French.* They grow only along the coastal plains and the nearby valleys of southern California, while the *French* group is resistant to greater extremes of both heat and cold and grows from central California to Oregon.

Neither of these English Walnuts will grow well in the southern states, and both need deep, well-drained, fertile soil to give best yield and quality. They also are sensitive to alkali salts and must have pure irrigation water.

The Walnut most likely to succeed in most parts of the United States is the Carpathian or Hardy English Walnut. This is the tree offered in most of the nursery catalogs, and it will grow and produce surprisingly well in colder climates. This hardy strain comes from the Carpathian Mountains of Eastern Europe where they grow and bear in spite of temperatures approaching thirty degrees below zero. The Reverend Paul C. Crath, a native of the region who had emigrated to Canada, returning to his homeland as a missionary became interested in the Walnuts he had known in his boyhood. When he came back to Canada once again he brought some of them with him.

Interest in these trees grew in the United States and a few thousand nuts were purchased for experimental growing. While these trees are still undergoing tests for variety selection, there now are many excellent named varieties to choose from and others are being developed.

The hardy Walnut also was established west of the Carpathians, in Poland, Czechoslovakia and central and southern Germany, where the summers were warm enough to permit the kernels to develop. German emigrants brought these to America during the early 1700's and made plantings in Pennsylvania and other states. Many descendants of these early trees still are flourishing on many American homesteads, and selected trees of this strain also are being used in experimental work for new varieties.

While the cold-hardy race of *Juglans regia*, broadly termed "Carpathian Walnut" is adapted to northern latitudes, the most successful plantings are made in Zone 6. They are limited in the extreme North by late fall freezes, extreme winter cold and cold injury in the spring. Fluctuating warm and cold spells also are detrimental to the trees. When fully dormant the Carpathian can withstand temperatures of -35° to -40° F., but it will be injured at 10° to 15° F. if cold follows upon a warm period during the winter. Sudden changes in the weather may cause trunk injury, and spring frosts often damage shoots and blossoms. This is because many varieties have buds which fail to remain dormant until danger of frost is passed. A cool or short summer also is a limiting factor, and there must be sufficient summer heat to mature the entire fruit. In such regions, only varieties able to mature nuts with well-filled kernels quickly should be planted.

Hansen is one of the best varieties. This is a comparatively small tree thought to be of German origin. It is an annual bearer of rather small, thin-shelled nuts but with the highest percentage of kernel of any variety. The trees are self-pollinating and adapted to a wide range.

Metcalfe, a Carpathian, is winter hardy in New York and is a good annual bearer of medium-sized nuts. *Somers* is an early-ripening variety and is a good choice for areas having cool or short summers. The medium-size nuts are well filled by early September in central Michigan. This variety apparently also is resistant to the husk maggot. *Broadview* is reputed to be the highest producer of any variety, though the flavor of the nuts is considered slightly bitter. *Burtner*, selected from Pennsylvania Dutch seedling trees of German origin, is an annual bearer of handsome nuts. Because it is late to "vegetate" (shed pollen) this variety has a good chance of escaping frost damage.

This list by no means exhausts the possibilities of the named varieties and more are being developed constantly. In the future, careful selection probably will permit cold-hardy Walnuts to be grown almost anywhere in the United States.

SPACING

The hardy Walnut will make a handsome landscape specimen for any yard. The open, globe-shaped head gives the tree a graceful, lofty appearance yet provides plenty of cool shade. The foliage also has a pleasing fragrance. It is a fine tree for a front lawn, since grass grows well under it. The tree, which attains an average height of 30 to 40 feet, will not dwarf a small house as some of the larger types tend to do.

With some varieties you may need to plant more than one to secure proper pollination for a larger nut crop. Some friends of mine solved this problem by planting a tree in their yard and suggesting that the neighbors on either side do the same. This was done and everybody profited, for these trees bear heavily in three to five years.

For the homestead where a full orchard may be planned it is advisable to space the trees at least 50 feet apart. Trees grafted on dwarfing interstocks, or a naturally small variety such as *Hansen,* may be planted as closely as 30 to 35 feet apart.

GRAFTED CARPATHIAN WALNUTS

(This does not represent a complete list of varieties available)

Variety	Size	Flavor
Hansen	Medium	Very Good
Helmle	Medium	Very Good
Merkel	Large	Very Good
Colby	Small	Very Good
Henry	Large	Very Good
James	Large	Very Good
Lake	Large	Very Good
McKinster	Large	Very Good
Fateley	Large	Very Good
Helmle No. 8	Large	Good
*Royal**	Extra Large	Good

FERTILIZING

The one element most necessary to the Carpathian Walnut throughout its range is nitrogen, while extra phosphorous and potash also are beneficial, especially with bearing trees. A soil analysis, particularly if you plan an extensive planting, will determine if such elements are deficient. Walnuts adapt best to a neutral or slightly acid soil. On a highly acid or heavily leached soil you may find an application of dolomitic or ground limestone is helpful.

PROPAGATION

Carpathian Walnuts like Pecans and many other nuts do not come true from seed and must be propagated vegetatively. Budding or grafting are the methods generally used, with the eastern Black Walnut as the stock apparently being most

*Note: *Royal* does not always fill well.

Cracking	Bearing	No. of Years
Excellent	Prolific	3-5 Yrs.
Excellent	Prolific	3-5 Yrs.
Excellent	Prolific	3-5 Yrs.
Excellent	Prolific	3-5 Yrs.
Excellent	Prolific	3-5 Yrs.
Excellent	Prolific	3-5 Yrs.
Excellent	Prolific	3-5 Yrs.
Excellent	Not yet determined	
Excellent	Prolific	3-5 Yrs.
Excellent	Prolific	3-5 Yrs.
Fair	Medium	3-5 Yrs.

compatible. Topworking your own trees from seedlings may be an interesting hobby, but grafting is somewhat more difficult with the Carpathian Walnuts than with other trees. If you plan to grow only a few trees, then, I would strongly advise purchasing varieties already grafted.

Nevertheless, if you want the tree only for landscape purposes, seedlings are easily grown and are just as attractive as grafted trees. Quite possibly the nuts will not be as good but, as with Pecans, every now and then a seedling tree will turn out well — perhaps even good enough to become a new "named" variety.

THE HARVEST

Another feature which makes the Carpathian Walnut an excellent landscape tree is their clean nut fall. Unlike the Black Walnut, the nuts usually fall free of their husks, permitting quick and easy gathering, or they may be raked together on the grass. The husks will wither and fall later with the leaves, but they provide no particular problems in disposal. One pound of nuts will yield about a half pound of nutmeats.

THE CARMELO WALNUT

For those who live in the western states, where the more tender varieties of Walnut can be grown, there is nothing quite like the *Carmelo*. This Walnut was developed and introduced by Sierra Gold Nurseries through a planned program to breed new and better Walnut varieties.

The *Carmelo* nut is BIG — are almost twice as large as the average Walnut — some even as large as small peaches — and the meats are huge, white and of superb quality. The tree, which leafs out in mid-spring and may be harvested in September, primarily is grown commercially, but also is most favored for home planting because of its vigorous growth and size. It grows to 60 feet in height and has a 40- to 60-foot spread. It is not recommended for small city lots but is excellent for large lots or suburban areas. Perhaps best of all, the *Carmelo* should bear the third year after planting. It has about the same range as the

English Walnut grown in California, and can stand temperatures down to 15 degrees above zero, but no lower.

Nursery Whip headed

TO PLANT THE CARMELO

The trees need good soil that is deep and well-drained. Dig your hole at least 24 inches in diameter and 30 inches deep, enlarging it if necessary to accommodate all the tree's root system without crowding. The tree should be set so that after settling it will be at about the same depth that it grew in the nursery — the place on the tree where the rough bark changes to the smooth root. Spread the roots naturally and fill the hole with loose dirt, firming the soil about the roots to eliminate air pockets, but not hard enough to pack. Don't trim the roots unless really necessary, and then trim only any broken or shredded roots or the extremely long ones that will not fit the hole.

Pruned at planting to reduce close branching and to form leader.

Do not fertilize when planting. Wait until the tree is in full leaf in late May or early June and then apply a moderate amount of a mixed fertilizer (about a half pound) by distributing it in a circle on the ground about a foot from the tree. You may do this two or three times during the summer and always before watering, which each time should be with enough water to penetrate six feet deep. The tree should receive sufficient irrigation during the spring and summer to prevent the soil from drying out, usually about every two weeks.

After the tree is set, cut back the top to about 15 inches above the bud union. Seal the top cut with tree wax. To prevent sunburn, wrap or whitewash the entire tree before the buds have opened.

Regrowth of laterals after heading

After the buds have opened and grown several inches in length, select the most vigorous and cut off all others. This will force the growth into the single bud that in time will form the tree. Cut the top of the tree back again to the remaining limb and wax the cut. It is a good idea to tie the tree about every 10 inches of height to a strong stake, placing the stake on the southwest side of the tree. This will aid in shading the tree and help to prevent sunburn.

If any suckers on the Black Walnut root stock appear, they should be cut off as often as necessary. Tree limbs should be allowed to form naturally from five feet or higher. If necessary,

Regrowth after heading

Well-spaced branches are unlikely to split.

Those close together often will split.

Scaffold branches with good vertical and radial spacing.

when the tree is seven or eight feet tall head it back once again to five or six feet above the ground to promote side limb development.

Vegetables will not grow well close to the *Carmelo* but spearmint will thrive and fruit mints such as apple, orange or pineapple also will do well nearby.

WALNUT PROBLEMS

Walnut trees grown where lawns or ornamentals require frequent watering, and those grown on Black Walnut roots particularly, are susceptible to crown rot. This is caused by a soil fungus that attacks the bark of the crown just below the soil surface, and is most likely to occur during the warm, growing season.

Dead areas appear first in the inner bark of the crown. These light-tan to black, soft and frequently spongy decayed areas are found in the bark at the base of the trunk and extend into the bark of the main roots. The diseased areas later may spread up the trunk and in English Walnuts sometimes invade the bark above the bud or graft union. Affected trees appear stunted, have sparse yellow foliage and little twig growth.

As a preventive, do not water within four feet of the trunk. This means that most ornamentals should not be planted around the tree, although you may use succulents or bulbs (that store up moisture from winter and spring rains) and above mentioned mints (that do not require much water during the dry season).

If you suspect crown rot, remove the soil and expose the crown, for if it girdles the crown or trunk the tree is doomed. Cut away some of the outer root bark to reveal any discolored, underlying inner bark. If it has not yet girdled the tree, removing soil from the base of the roots and the trunk allows the crown to dry and usually arrests a further spread. Early attention often can save the life of an affected tree if the disease has not progressed too far. If crown rot threatens, it is best to leave the hole open for at least one year, providing drainage from the hole during the rainy season.

You also can cut out the rotted bark on the trunk and cover the exposed wood with Bordeaux paint. Bark below the soil surface on crown and roots usually is thin enough so it is not necessary to remove it to achieve effective aeration.

After the immediate danger is past, you can fill the hole with stones, to maintain air circulation to prevent recurrence of crown rot, but never apply water within four feet of the trunk. For clay soils, lawns and areas with excessive moisture, the Sierra Gold Nurseries recommend *Carmelo* on Paradox root which has greater resistance to crown rot.

A bacterial disease, Walnut blight, does not harm the tree but can damage the nuts. Darkened areas on the hulls, especially near the blossom end, may indicate the problem. Spraying is recommended to prevent the blight. Do this during the early pre-bloom stage when about one percent of the pistillate blooms have opened for pollination.

Walnut aphids suck out large amounts of sap and give off honey-dew on which a black, sooty fungus grows. If not controlled they can considerably lessen kernel quality and nut size. Control them with one pint of 50-percent malathion liquid emulsive concentrate per 100 gallons of water.

For leaf-chewing caterpillars apply malathion or Sevin. Scale insects can be controlled by spraying in January or February (in the South) with three gallons of dormant grade oil emulsion per 100 gallons of water.

For Walnut husk fly spray with malathion which kills the adult before she can lay eggs. However, the spray cannot kill the eggs or larvae once they are deposited in the husk, so it is necessary to make repeated applications.

Exposing the crown controls crown rot.

WALNUT RECIPES

walnut zucchini bread

1 cup Walnuts
4 eggs
2 cups sugar
1 cup vegetable oil
3½ cups unsifted, unbleached flour
1½ tsp. baking soda
2 tsp. salt
1 teaspoon cinnamon
½ teaspoon allspice
¾ teaspoon baking powder
2 cups grated zucchini
    (Golden zucchini if possible)
1 cup raisins
1 teaspoon vanilla

Chop Walnuts coarsely. Beat eggs, gradually adding sugar. Beat in oil. Combine dry ingredients and add to first mixture alternately with zucchini. Add raisins, Walnuts and vanilla. Bake in two oiled and lightly floured loaf pans at 350° F. for about 50 minutes, or until loaves test done. Cooled loaves may be lightly glazed with confectioner's sugar mixed to spreading consistency with a little orange juice.

walnut poultry stuffing

Giblets from 1 fowl
1 onion chopped
1 bay leaf
1 cup boiling water
½ pound bread crumbs
1 tablespoon salt
2 tablespoons poultry seasoning or sage
2 cups chopped Walnuts
4 tablespoons cooking oil

Cook giblets, onion and bay leaf in boiling water until tender. Remove bay leaf, drain giblets and chop finely. Add remaining ingredients and toss together lightly. Moisten with giblet stock. This stuffing will fill a 12 to 14 pound fowl.

meat loaf with walnut stuffing

1½ pounds beef, ground
½ cup chopped green pepper
¾ cup chopped onion
1½ tsp. salt
1 tablespoon Worcestershire sauce
1 cup bread crumbs, white
½ cup milk
¼ cup oil
2 eggs
½ cup chopped celery
½ cup chopped Walnuts
¼ tsp. pepper
¾ cup water or meat stock
2 cups whole-wheat bread crumbs

Combine beef, green pepper, ½ cup of onion, salt, Worcestershire sauce, white bread crumbs, milk and one egg. Mix thoroughly. Place ½ mixture in bottom of oiled loaf pan. Combine all remaining ingredients, mix thoroughly and place on top of meat mixture. Add remaining meat mixture on top of stuffing. Bake at 350° F. about 1½ hours. Cool slightly and serve.

walnut-fig loaf

2 cups sifted, unbleached flour
1 teaspoon salt
4 teaspoons baking powder
1/3 cup sugar
1 cup whole-wheat or graham
    flour
1 cup toasted English Walnuts
    coarsely chopped
½ cup dried figs, chopped fine
1 egg
1½ cups milk

Sift first 4 ingredients together. Mix in whole-wheat flour, nuts and figs. Beat egg slightly and add milk. Add liquid to dry ingredients, stirring just enough to dampen the flour. Pour into greased loaf pan and bake in moderate oven (350° F.) one hour.

Walnuts are very easy to crack, but you will get more whole nutmeats if you first place them in a large bowl and cover with lightly salted water. Use one tablespoon of salt to each two quarts of water and let them stand overnight. Drain and dry with paper towels. The shells can then be easily pried apart with a screwdriver, I use a small, short-handled screwdriver, about five inches long.

7

CHESTNUTS & CHINKAPINS

Everybody who writes about Chestnuts begins by telling all about the blight of the American Chestnut — so let's get it over with.

The Chestnut blight fungus, *Endothia parasitica*, discovered in the New York City Zoological Park in 1904, is believed to have come from northeast Asia on imported Asiatic Chestnut trees. The infection spread rapidly from New York to New England, and less than fifty years later, carried by birds, insects and the wind, the spores of the deadly fungus had reached every part of the Chestnut's natural range, and an estimated nine million acres of Chestnut forests were killed. No cure has yet been found, so you can't grow the American Chestnuts — and that's that.

What we are concerned with here is the Chestnut *(Castanea)* which we *can* grow, the blight-resistant Chinese *(C. mollissima)*. And if you like Chestnuts and want to grow them you need not feel short-changed, for the Chinese indeed are of superior eating quality, far better than any of the imported cooking Chestnuts.

The tree, too, is beautiful and spreading with a rounded top, is as cold-hardy as the Peach, and is suited to nut production over a wide range of climate and soil conditions. It will withstand -20° *F. temperatures when fully dormant and is very long-lived. The standard varieties, Nanking, Meriling, Kuling* and *Abundance,* are the most popular, while *Orrin* and *Crane* also are excellent choices.

It is another bonus that this tree can be grown in a limited space. Perhaps best of all, the spiny burs assure the grower of a squirrel-proof nut crop. It would be a daring bushy-tail indeed that tried to rob this tree of its nuts before it is ready to let them drop.

Actually the Chinese Chestnut is a bit *hardier* than the Peach, growing well in Zones 8 to 4, which includes most of the continental United States, but it is less tolerant of humid, tropical areas. If you happen to live in Florida grow something else — like maybe the Macadamia.

Again like Peaches, Chinese Chestnuts bear young, and even may give a small crop of nuts the second year after planting. A friend who is president of one of the leading nurseries told me that the Chestnuts he sells will produce a sure crop the second year, and sometimes will yield the first year they are planted. He went on to say, "In the spring we line out our surplus stock, and almost every fall we can go out and pick a few Chestnuts from that stock planted in late spring. By about the fourth year you're getting meaningful production."

Chestnuts will grow reasonably well on average-type soils, good drainage being more important to them than high fertility. Sandy soil tending toward the acid is a good choice. Hillsides often make good Chestnut ground and, unlike many other trees, they even will grow in gravelly or stony soil. But eroded slopes should be avoided.

This does not mean that Chestnuts will not benefit from really good soil. A tree located in deep, alluvial soil (sedimentary earth containing organic matter) will produce more and nearly twice as large nuts as those from a tree growing in eroded soil having a shallow hardpan. Tree nutrition *is* important.

Nut size, however, is a variable factor influenced not only by environment but by the age of the tree. Young trees generally bear larger nuts (but fewer of them) than an older tree of the same variety. Nut size even may vary on the same tree, heavily laden branches bearing smaller nuts than those on a branch with only a few burs. But your trees will benefit from feeding them barnyard manure and compost, while mulching with hay or leaves also will help.

CROSS-POLLINATION

Chestnuts are practically self-sterile, so you will need two or more trees to produce nuts. Without cross-pollination individual trees may develop burs without kernels. On a 40-foot spacing, pairs of Chestnut trees should not be planted more than 60 feet from each other because pollen is largely insect-carried, although the wind also plays a part if trees are near enough together.

Sometimes limited space problems can be solved by neighbors each planting one of a pair. If you have plenty of land area you can plant several seedlings.

In Europe clump plantings of nut crops is a common practice. Sometimes, as with Filberts, several seedlings are put in the same hole to assure proper pollination. I do not advise this practice, but it is a possibility and sometimes can solve the space problem.

CHESTNUTS FROM SEED

Chestnuts are reproduced from seed or by grafting older trees with scions removed from last season's growth. As with most other types of nuts grafted trees begin bearing at an earlier age and produce better nuts.

So far grafting has proven to be the best means of propagating Chestnuts. Other means such as hardwood cuttings and air layering have not been satisfactory. Grafting must be done carefully, and as a general rule rootstocks for varieties of Chinese Chestnuts should be seedlings of the same species. Otherwise the graft may prove to be incompatible. If you want only a few trees I would advise buying already grafted trees from a reliable nursery.

Growing Chestnuts from seed is not difficult, and may be the answer if you want a number of trees. A few seedlings growing among your grafted trees also provide additional opportunities for cross-pollination. Hybrid seed *(Manchurian x American)* is obtainable from Earl Douglas, Red Creek, N.Y. 13143.

The seeds need a storage treatment of at least one to two months at 32 to 36° F. This will break the embryo dormancy and insure uniform germination. But do not subject the stored seed to temperatures much below freezing or above 45° F.

Chestnut seed is started preferably in the spring, as fall planting is a bit of a gamble with squirrels and mice. You can store seed nuts until spring in clay pots filled with sand and peat moss and (unless your winters are very cold) buried under garden litter in a protective wire covering.

Plant your seeds point down about a half inch deep and two inches apart. Since moisture is very essential for the first several years, seedlings are most easily cared for in a coldframe. A heavy mulch also will help moisture retention as well as discourage competitive vegetation. Given favorable conditions, trees may make as much as 10 feet of growth in ten years. The average height of a mature Chestnut is between 40 and 50 feet. Sometimes seedlings will begin bearing as early as their 5th year.

If you do decide to graft your seedlings the most satisfactory method is the splice graft, using scion and stock of approximately the same diameter. Whip grafting also may be practiced.

For a graft to be successful there are two important conditions to consider: First, allow the rootstock to leaf out fully; second, use dormant scionwood. Do not graft too early in the spring or the buds on the graft stock may start into early growth and possibly be killed by a late spring frost.

PRUNING

The Chinese Chestnut should be pruned very little since cutting will endanger the productive crown. Branches should be removed during the dormant season if they are dead or crowding. Sometimes, after a prolonged drought, dead branch tips will become noticeable.

FLOWERING

One of the reasons Chinese Chestnuts are so desirable is their habit of flowering late, which practically eliminates crop failure from frost. In Washington, D.C. the slender, erect catkins flower in early June, farther north around the first part of July.

The flowers, which are borne on the current season's shoots, are produced on two kinds of catkins. The long, finger-like staminate or male catkin, located on the lower portion of the shoot, are the first to flower. The female or pistillate flowers are located at the base of one or more bisexual catkins and are near the upper portion of the shoot. Not all trees have the same sequence of bloom of the staminate and pistillate flowers, but the pattern of flower maturity is distinctive with each tree or variety and it is constant each season.

Proper fertilization usually results in a neat package of three nuts nestled in a protective, spiny bur where they remain invulnerable until the burs open to release the ripe fruit. Chinese Chestnuts generally begin dropping in late September or early October.

TO HARVEST AND STORE

Curing conditions greatly affect the quality of Chestnuts. The freshly-harvested kernels mostly contain starch and almost no sugar, but as the nuts lose moisture the sugar content increases. You can tell when a Chestnut is properly cured: It will feel slightly soft when pressed between the thumb and forefinger. The chemical changes that take place as the nut cures is not fully understood, but quality certainly is influenced by the method of handling and storing.

Fresh Chestnuts contain 40 to 45 percent carbohydrates, mostly in the form of starch, five percent oil and about 50 percent moisture. Since they lose moisture rapidly they are highly perishable and also may be attacked by fungus and bacteria.

Chestnuts have a wide range in keeping quality, varying from one tree to another, with varieties such as *Crane* and *Orrin* being considered among the best keepers. The attractive nuts of *Crane* are a deep cherry-red while the *Orrin* are a rich, dark mahogany.

Harvest the nuts at least every other day, and do not allow them to lie in the sun, for this will bring about rapid deterioration of the kernel. Place the nuts in polyethylene bags or ventilated cans to allow for the escape of moisture. You even may mix dry peat moss with the nuts to absorb moisture. Proper curing is important, for as the starches are changed to sugar the eating quality is greatly improved. Their best storage temperature is 32 to 36° F.

The soft shell of the Chestnut is removed easily by peeling it with a sharp knife. Make the first cut across the base of the nut. If the nuts are first boiled in water for three or four minutes the shell and pellicle (a thin skin or film) come off even more easily. The kernels then are ready to be cooked or otherwise used for eating. One pound of shelled Chestnuts will yield about two-and-a-half cups of nutmeats.

ROASTING CHESTNUTS

How well I remember my first attempt to roast Chestnuts. I knew nothing about the proper method, so I just put them in a shallow pan and set them in the oven turned to low heat. The first warning of disaster was a loud popping noise followed by another and then another. I rushed into the kitchen, opened the oven door and stared. The nuts had exploded like miniature firecrackers and there was Chestnut *all over the place!*

Don't let this happen to you. Slit the shells before roasting whole Chestnuts to prevent the shell from bursting. A crisscross gash on the flat side is easiest.

Here is another trick with Chestnuts. With a sharp knife make a slit in each. Place in boiling water and boil for 3 or 4 minutes. Remove and dry thoroughly. Melt 3 tablespoons of butter or margarine in a saucepan, add the Chestnuts and heat, stirring thoroughly until very hot. Then with a sharp-pointed knife, both skins can be removed together, leaving the nut whole. Or if you like, roast the scored nuts in a very hot oven (450° F.) about 10 to 15 minutes.

Boiled or roasted Chestnuts, with the shells removed, may be placed in heavy plastic bags and frozen. They will keep almost indefinitely and are handy to use for many recipes.

Chestnuts are considered by many to *be* a vegetable — not merely to be used *with* vegetables.

CHESTNUT RECIPES

chestnut stuffing

1½ pound loaf of bread, dried
½ to 1 cup cooking oil
1 tsp. salt
½ tsp. pepper
½ cup minced onion
2 tablespoons poultry seasoning
1 pound Chestnuts cooked and chopped
Cut sliced bread into one-inch cubes. Toss all ingredients together lightly. Stuffing may be baked in an oiled ring mold or loaf pan if you do not want to bake it in the fowl or meat. When stuffing is removed from ring mold, hot cooked vegetables may be placed in the center.

duck with chestnuts

3 pound duck
2 cups boiling water
6 cups Chestnuts
2 cups sliced mushrooms
1 tsp. salt
¼ tsp. pepper
4 tablespoons soy sauce
Cut duck into serving portions, cover with hot water and simmer for one hour (or until tender). Drop Chestnuts into cold water and discard any which float. Heat water to boiling and simmer Chestnuts 5 to 6 minutes. Drain and peel. Add Chestnuts, mushrooms, salt, pepper and soy sauce to duck and simmer 30 minutes longer. Very good served with rice.

chestnuts and sweet potatoes

6 medium sweet potatoes
1 pound Chestnuts
½ cup brown sugar
¼ cup hot water
¼ cup margarine
½ cup buttered bread crumbs
½ tsp. cinnamon
¼ tsp. nutmeg

Wash, pare and slice potatoes. Boil 5 minutes and drain. Wash Chestnuts and discard any that float. Shell and simmer in boiling water (to cover) until tender, 8 to 15 minutes. Drain. Place potatoes and Chestnuts in alternate layers in an oiled casserole. Boil together brown sugar, hot water, cinnamon, nutmeg and margarine. Pour over potatoes. Cover with bread crumbs. Bake in moderate oven (350° F.) until potatoes are tender.

chestnut freeze

4 egg yolks
¼ cup sugar
½ cup top milk or cream
2 tablespoons rum or brandy
1 cup heavy cream, whipped
1 cup ground Chestnuts
1 cup Graham cracker crumbs
¼ tsp. mace

Beat egg yolks, add sugar, mace and top milk. Cook over hot water 5 minutes stirring constantly until thickened. Chill. Add rum or brandy and fold into whipped cream. Pour a half inch layer of cream mixture in bottom of a freezing tray. Sprinkle with a layer of ground Chestnuts and a layer of cracker crumbs. Repeat until all ingredients are used. Freeze until firm.

chestnut puree

3 cups Chestnuts, roasted
4 cups chicken broth
½ tsp. salt
⅛ tsp. pepper
2 cups cream or rich milk
Roast Chestnuts, take from oven and remove shells and skins
with a sharp knife. Add Chestnuts to broth and cook until soft.
Rub nuts through a coarse sieve and return to broth. Add salt,
pepper and milk. Reheat and serve with toasted croutons.

chestnut stroganoff

1½ pounds beef, boneless, tender,
    lean, cut in julienne strips
1 tablespoon fat or oil
2 tablespoons butter or margarine
2 tablespoons all purpose flour
½ teaspoon onion salt
½ teaspoon celery salt
½ teaspoon paprika
¼ teaspoon salt
1¼ cups beef bouillon
    or beef broth
½ cup sour cream
1 tablespoon cooking sherry
1 cup Chestnuts, cooked, mashed (see note)
Baked potatoes or cooked rice or noodles, as desired

Lightly brown the meat in fat or oil in a frying pan over
moderate heat. Drain off any excess fat. Melt butter or margarine
in saucepan. Blend in flour and seasonings. Add bouillon or
broth slowly, stirring constantly. Stir and cook until smooth
and bubbly. Remove from heat. Blend in sour cream, sherry and
Chestnuts. Add Chestnut sauce to meat. Heat just until mixture
bubbles, stirring constantly. Serve over potatoes, rice or noodles.

Note: To prepare mashed Chestnuts: Cook 1¼ cups boiling
water in a covered saucepan for about 30 minutes or until
tender. Drain and mash.

CHINKAPINS

The Chinkapins (or Chinquapins) are the little brothers of the Chestnut, distinguished by having only one nut per bur instead of three. The nuts also are much smaller but are very sweet and good.

Chinkapins grow to be medium-sized trees in Texas and Arkansas, but east of the Mississippi are progressively smaller, often becoming mere scrubby undergrowth east of the Alleghenies. Here they cover rocky banks or crouch along swamp borders.

In leaf, flower and fruit Chinkapins are much like their big brothers, but are much more resistant to the Chestnut blight fungus. Though not immune, they usually compensate for the loss of a diseased stem by increased growth of the remaining stems and send up vigorous new shoots.

All of the small trees or shrubs bear young, usually at three to five years of age. Unless they occur naturally on their home grounds Chinkapins seldom are cultivated, but they do provide a very valuable source of food for wildlife.

The Allegheny Chinkapin *(C. pumila)*, is the most common and is hardy in Zone 6, growing about 10 feet tall as a prolific producer of the small, sweet "Chestnuts." The leaves have a mat of wooly, white hairs on the undersides, the burs (about one-inch in diameter) are spherical, and the spines are much softer than other species. The little trees are quite ornamental.

The Ozark Chinkapin *(C. ozarkensis)* will make a small tree but is seen most often as a multi-stemmed shrub. It occurs naturally in Arkansas, Oklahoma and Missouri and also is hardy in Zone 6. The quite small nuts are chiefly valuable as a food for wildlife, but are good to eat if you have the patience to hull them.

The Louis Gerardi Nursery has an improved variety, the *American Hybrid "A,"*, which produces medium-size nuts with very good flavor and good cracking quality. This Chinquapin bears very young (two to three years), and is very prolific.

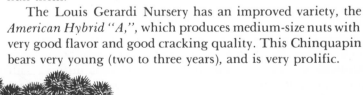

8

FILBERTS OR HAZELNUTS

Filberts need two to tango, but they are very gregarious and also obliging. They present a distinct advantage for the homeowner with very little space. Even though they require two varieties to produce, in a pinch you can plant both in the same hole.

Filberts make excellent hedges when grown in bush form or they may be trained by careful pruning into small trees. Generally speaking "Filbert" applies to domesticated varieties, the term "Hazelnut" to the wild ones. The European Filbert, (*Corylus avellana*) is the only species cultivated extensively for its nuts, though about 15 *Corylus* species are recognized. The nuts of this variety are very large compared to the others, and the plants grow naturally as a shrub 15 feet or more in height. In some areas under favorable conditions and when trained to tree form they even may grow as large as apple trees. Some nurseries offer a dwarf species which grows only four feet tall in shrub form. The clustered nuts are slightly smaller but have the same grand flavor.

Filberts are delicious and always are found in the best nut

mixtures. They form in compact clusters, each nut encased in its own husk around the smooth, hard, but thin and brittle shell. The kernels are single, and when the shell is cracked most of the tasty meats may be removed whole.

Filberts are accommodating in other ways, too. They need no special soil or site requirements beyond those essential for other fruit or nut trees. The plants *do not have long taproots.* Therefore, transplanting is much easier than with most other nut trees.

FERTILIZER REQUIREMENTS

Filberts often will do reasonably well on poor soil, but health and harvests can be improved if certain needs are met. They are most likely to be responsive to moderate nitrogen applications, but too much will stimulate the plants into lush growth and they will be more liable to winter injury. Observe your plants. If the leaves are large and dark green the supply of nitrogen is good. If they are small and yellowish there is a deficiency. On light soils there may be a potash deficiency, but a soil test will give the answer if your plants are not doing well.

WHERE TO PLANT

A northern slope is preferable because this will delay blooming, which should not occur if possible until temperatures lower than 15° are no longer expected. Filberts should not be planted in warm, sheltered spots near buildings or on southern slopes, but shelter from prevailing winds *is* desirable.

PRUNING

Prune your trees at planting time just as you would a fruit tree. It should be headed at two feet above the ground with four to six scaffold branches well distributed so as to avoid the formation of weak crotches. This is all that will be necessary. Until bearing age pruning should be light and corrective only.

Filberts bear their nuts laterally and terminally on wood of the previous season's growth. After the tree has come into bearing, pruning should be just sufficient to stimulate a moderate amount of new growth each year. A minimum amount of thinning without heading back is all that's needed. Prune your Filberts just as you would Peaches but less severely, since too much may result in winter killing. Prune at the close of the blooming period, right after the catkins have shed their pollen.

Some varieties tend to sucker profusely and if these are not removed you will have a bush instead of a tree with a single stem, which many find the easiest form to manage and the most desirable. So if you want a tree, you must subdue the suckers as they appear. Older trees will produce progressively fewer suckers.

PROPAGATION

Filberts may be raised easily from seeds, but the varieties do not come true, so that layering, easily accomplished, is much more satisfactory. This has a distinct advantage too, since the Filberts grow on their own roots and the variety will not be lost if the plant is winter injured.

If you want only a few new plants you may mound soil up around suckers in the spring to a depth of several inches. By the following year roots will have developed at the base of the sucker, which then may be taken up and placed in a nursery row or in a new location.

Another easy method of propagation is "simple layering." This is done by bending a branch to the ground in a V-shape and pegging it down to the bottom of a trench to a depth of five or six inches. Do this in the spring just as growth is starting. The tip of the shoot, which should be upright, will continue to grow, forming a new plant.

Simple Layering: Bend a branch to the ground, covering part 5 to 10 inches from tip with compost.

It will help matters along if the soil around the parent tree or bush is prepared before layering. This is best done by working in sand, peat moss or compost to lighten and condition the soil. It is important, too, that the medium in which the layer is rooted be well drained, have good aeration and still be capable of holding moisture.

Girdle the branch before covering it with soil by removing a ring of bark about one inch wide from the portion you plan to cover. Another way is to wound it by making a knife cut about half way through the stem on the lower surface. Wounding done in this manner speeds up rooting, which will be even faster if the wound is treated with a root-inducing hormone powder. The layer will stay firmly held in place if pegged down with a piece of heavy, U-shaped wire or a forked branch.

Layering may be done in spring, using dormant wood produced during the previous growing season. Start as early as possible, being sure to keep the moisture supply sufficient so that rooting will be encouraged. Layering may also be done in late summer using the current season's growth which is still supple. Again be sure there is adequate moisture.

If the spring-rooted plant is well grown by fall and with a good root system developed, it may be cut free and transplanted either into a nursery row or a new location. But where winters are severe it often is better to leave the rooted layer attached to the parent plant until the following spring.

Use only young and vigorous plants for layering since older plants create too much shade and competition for moisture and nutrients.

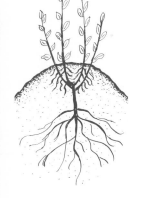

Mound Layering: Cut shrub back to encourage growth of suckers, which will root when mounded with earth.

POLLINATION

Filberts are monoecious: the male and female flowers are borne separately on the same plant (as with corn), and the pollen is transferred by the wind. All Filbert varieties require cross pollination — *Royal* and *Barcelona* (Burgess Seed & Nursery Company) are excellent companions — and every planting should have two or more varieties.

As previously mentioned, if space is at a premium two even may be planted in the same hole. You may expect better results, however, if trees are planted about 15 feet apart. In the South Filberts start blooming about the middle of March. Shelter from north and west winds, that damage the pollen-bearing catkins, is always desirable in a northern planting.

HARVESTING AND STORING

Filberts are harvested by picking after they drop to the ground. Nut shells, at the time of harvest, are of a yellowish-red-brown color known the world over as "hazel." Remember the girl with the "nut-brown hair?" When the nuts are dry it is best to store them in an unheated building where outside temperatures and humidities prevail. Kept at room temperature they soon become rancid.

As with Pecans and many other nuts I prefer to crack Filberts as soon as they are dry and then refrigerate or freeze them. You may expect two-and-a-half pounds of Filberts in the shell to yield about one pound of nutmeats, equal to about three-and-a-half cups.

Filberts are almost indescribably delicious and have been considered a gastronomic delight, wherever they were known, since at least 1000 B.C. Their faintly sweet flavor makes them superb for baking. They are light and fluffy when ground. They combine well with many other flavors, are particularly good with chocolate, and are no less desirable when used with meat or poultry or even fish, excellent in stuffings, sauces and butters. If you decide to grow Filberts you are in for a real treat, not just once but many times.

For baking purposes I prefer to leave the skins *un*blanched which I think adds a great deal of flavor. However, shelled nuts may be toasted (or roasted) by spreading in a single layer in an ungreased pie tin or on a baking sheet. Preheat oven to 350° F. and toast for about 15 minutes, or to just golden brown, stirring occasionally so they will brown evenly, being careful not to overroast. As they cool rub the nuts vigorously with a clean cloth.

Filberts are just great for a snack or appetizer when merely toasted, buttered and very lightly salted. I like to use the very finely ground popcorn salt for nuts.

FILBERT RECIPES

filbert stuffing

¼ cup butter or margarine
¼ cup onion, finely chopped
¼ cup celery (stalks and leaves)
    chopped
¼ cup mushrooms chopped
1 teaspoon salt
½ teaspoon thyme
¼ teaspoon poultry seasoning
Dash cayenne pepper
Dash garlic salt
2 cups bread cubes or coarse,
    soft crumbs
½ cup chicken or beef bouillon
    or meat broth
¾ cup Filberts, finely chopped

Preheat oven to 325° F. (slow). Grease a one-quart baking dish. Melt fat in a heavy pan. Add onion, celery, mushrooms, and seasonings. Cook a few minutes until celery is tender but still crisp, stirring occasionally. Add bread, bouillon or broth, and nuts. Mix lightly but well. Put stuffing into baking dish. Bake 25 to 30 minutes or until slightly browned. Or stuffing may be used as a filling for breast of chicken or veal or lamb.

sundae nut syrup

2 tablespoons butter or margarine
½ cup Filberts, blanched and chopped
¼ cup brown sugar, packed
2 tablespoons water
2 tablespoons light corn syrup

Melt fat in a small frying pan. Add nuts and cook over low heat, stirring as needed until nuts are lightly browned. Stir in remaining ingredients. Simmer two minutes. Serve warm over ice cream.

nut meringue shells

¼ teaspoon cream of tartar
3 egg whites
¼ teaspoon salt
¾ cup sugar
1 cup Filberts, chopped

Preheat oven to 250° F. (very slow). Add cream of tartar to egg whites and beat until foamy. Add salt and continue beating until soft peaks form. Add sugar gradually, beating constantly, until very stiff peaks form. Fold in chopped nuts. Drop meringue in six or 12 mounds, as desired, onto heavy brown paper or aluminum foil on a baking sheet. Using the back of a spoon, form a hollow in the center of each mound. Bake one hour. Turn off heat and let meringues cool in oven (one-and-a-half hours). Serve filled with iced cream or a cooled pudding.

curried nuts and fruit

1 can (1 lb. 13 oz.) peach halves
1 can (1 lb. 13 oz.) pear halves
1 can (1 lb. 4 oz.) pineapple chunks
5 maraschino cherries, sliced
¾ cup Filberts, coarsely
    chopped
1/3 cup butter or margarine
¾ cup brown sugar, packed
2 to 4 teaspoons curry powder

Drain fruit and place in heat-proof casserole or skillet. Add Filberts. Melt butter, add brown sugar and curry powder. Spread mixture on top of fruit and nuts. Heat over low flame or in 350° F. oven 20-25 minutes or until bubbly. Serve as an accompaniment to meat or fowl.

9

THE ALLURING ALMOND

This peculiar kind of Peach has a thick skin, almost no pulp or juice and a stone with a large kernel that is not bitter like the seed in a true Peach.

The Almond *(Prunus amygdalus)*, like many of our most important fruit plants, is a member of the Rose family, which also includes the apple, cherry, pear, peach, quince, loquat, plum, apricot and prune as well as many bramble fruits.

This odd kind of Peach apparently originated in southeastern Asia where it grew wild along with Pistachio shrubs in the scrub oak forests of such countries as Iraq, Jordan and Turkey. Both bitter and sweet Almonds have been cultivated in the Mediterranean area since before recorded history.

The earliest Almond trees in the United States were those grown from seed introduced from Mexico and Spain when the missions were established in California. But these trees died out after the missions were abandoned.

No further attempt was made to grow Almonds in the United States until 1840 when trees imported from Europe were planted in New England. But here the climate was too severe, and the attempt was not successful.

In time plantings were made down the length of the Atlantic seaboard and into the Gulf States, but everywhere the Amond's exacting climatic requirements ruled it out as a profitable crop.

In 1843 Almond trees brought from the East Coast were planted in California, which now is the only important Almond-producing state in the country. But in many areas of that state, too, they cannot be grown successfully.

The problem with Almonds isn't the trees, which are very hardy, but with the tenderness of blossoms and their tendency to bloom early. The flower of the Almond is similar to that of the Peach — in fact even may be fertilized by Peach trees that bloom at the same time. However, Almonds bloom *very* early. Even in February the branches may be covered with a breathtaking display of pink and white beauty, and it is this early-flowering habit that makes them susceptible to frost injury.

The flowers are perfect, (containing both stamens and pistils), the buds produced singly on the sides of short spurs, but under good conditions they may develop laterally on relatively long shoots.

All Almond varieties require pollen from another variety to produce a crop, and honey bees pollinate them as they go from flowers of one variety to those of another. So in an Almond orchard effective pollination depends on the weather, plant competition, bee colony strength and good management practiced by the grower and beekeeper.

In California the *Nonpareil* is considered the best all-around Almond because of high kernel quality, paper shell and high kernel-shell ratio. It is the most widely adaptable variety from the standpoint of marketing, and generally makes up the largest part of the orchard. All other varieties are normally considered as pollenizers for the *Nonpareil*.

Those of us who live in the eastern and central sections of the United States cannot successfully grow the California Almonds because of the frost hazard and the possible occurrence of rain and high humidity during the growing season. Newer, later blooming varieties are being tested which may prove worthwhile, but as yet the results are not conclusive.

Hall's Hardy Almond is the variety most frequently offered by nurseries for more northern sections, and it is grown to a limited extent as a tree for the home grounds. It can be grown successfully because it is relatively late blooming and doesn't require cross-pollinization. Generally speaking this Almond will do well wherever Peaches can be grown successfully. The Peach-like shell is hard and the kernel is slightly bitter. However many people prize this Almond and think it especially flavorful in baked goods.

This Hardy Almond with lovely pink blossoms in the spring, makes a beautiful lawn tree, growing 15 to 25 feet tall, and many think it worth planting for its beauty alone. It bears young, often within two to three years, and the nuts are large.

SOILS

Almonds will grow well on a wide variety of soils, from the finest valley loams to the rocky soils of the foothills. They grow and produce best, however, in deep, well-drained loam. In deep soils an Almond tree's roots will extend to a depth of 12 feet, but they extract most of their nutrients and moisture from the top six feet of soil. The trees will not do well in heavy or poorly drained soils and should not be planted in such locations.

PLANTING

It usually is best to get the trees as whips — just as they grew in the nursery — and to head them back after they are planted. When your trees arrive from the nursery do not allow the roots to dry out or become exposed to freezing temperatures. If you cannot plant immediately, heel-in the trees in damp soil or damp sawdust, but avoid covering the trunks of the trees above the depth at which they grew in the nursery. If the soil remains too wet to plant for long periods sometimes it is necessary to put the trees in cold storage until planting is possible.

Plant the trees very high because they will settle a good deal after planting, perhaps several inches, and this may lead to crown or collar rot. You can avoid this usually by being careful to dig the hole no deeper than necessary. Plant the trees so that the uppermost roots are just below the soil surface. There will still be some settling, but when the holes are refilled the trees should be at just about the proper depth. In any event, never plant the trees deeper than they grew in the nursery. Plant them, also, so that the bud is on the southwest side of the tree. This will help to reduce sunburn on the stock.

PLANTING DISTANCE

Almond trees (if you are growing more than one) ordinarily are placed 25 to 30 feet apart. Regardless of the distance between trees, a hexagonal planting (or triangle) will give about 17 percent more trees per acre than planting at the same distance on the square.

In orchard planting at left, in the hexagonal or triangle system, trees are 30 feet apart or 56 per acre. In orchard at right, planted on the square (trees and rows 30 feet apart), you can fit 48 per acre.

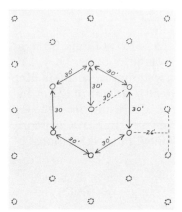
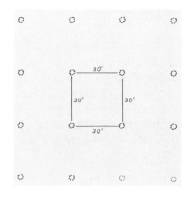

IRRIGATION

If you plant trees in moist soil during spring rains, watering usually isn't needed after planting.

If the soil is dry or rain is not imminent, settle the trees in the soil by applying water at planting time. If you irrigate after planting, fill the holes about three-quarters full with soil and then fill the rest with water. As soon as the water disappears, fill the hole with soil to ground level.

If you settle the soil around a tree with water, do not firm it further by stepping on it. This will compact the soil and may interfere with water penetration around the base of the tree and with normal root development. But when using this method take care that the planted trees do not settle too deeply in the soil.

It will be necessary to supply some water to the trees during the first year. The irrigation should be light and frequent, particularly for shallow or sandy soils. Trees planted in deep, mellow soil will require less irrigation provided the area is kept weed-free to eliminate competition for water. Under such conditions, the trees will get most of their water from the expanding root system as it explores new soil.

FERTILIZING TREES THE FIRST YEAR

Almonds benefit from light applications of nitrogen fertilizers during their first growing season. You can place the fertilizer in a furrow or broadcast it around the tree if you irrigate by sprinkler.

PEST CONTROL

No Almond variety is perfect, and even the *Nonpareil* is subject to noninfectious bud failure and bacterial canker. Almonds sometimes suffer from the same insects as Peach trees — Peach twig borer, spider mites, brown Almond mite and several types of plant bugs.

Garlic in a circle around your trees will foil the borers, dormant oil spray or commercial miticides are helpful against mites, or you can make a mixture of ground garlic, onions and hot peppers. Allow it to steep overnight in water, strain and use as a spray. Eradication programs should be started as soon as you detect the presence of any insect pests to prevent spreading.

TO TRAIN YOUR TREE

The way to get the biggest leaf and fruiting area on a tree in the shortest length of time is to do no pruning. Then, why prune trees? Here are some of the reasons: to obtain a vigorous and mechanically strong tree; to shape the tree for convenience and economy in management; to get good distribution of the fruiting area over the tree; to plan for a succession of good crops.

THE YOUNG TREE

The first pruning should take place when you plant your Almond. At this time cut back or head the tree to the height at which you wish to have the permanent branches arise.

Growers head their trees at a height of from 24 to 32 inches. The homeowner who will not use mechanical means of harvesting may train his tree a little higher or lower according to his personal preference.

In addition to heading your tree, cut back any small side shoots or branches but do not cut them off entirely, since you may have trouble later on finding new shoots that are well placed for permanent scaffold branches. So leave at least one base bud on each shoot.

A tree uses energy to grow branches. So if unneeded branches are left until after the season's growth, that energy is largely wasted. Pinch unwanted branches back when they are only a few inches long and the tree's vigor will be directed to the permenent branches.

With this in mind you can do a certain amount of summer pruning. Examine your tree when new growth is about three to four inches long. Select the shoots you wish to remain for scaffold branches and pinch back all others, leaving a few leaves to shade the trunk. Check again in four to six weeks to make sure that no new undesirable shoots are growing.

If the shoots selected for future scaffolds grow very vigorously, pinch off the ends when they are about 30 inches from the trunk. This will cause the shoots to branch.

By careful summer training you will greatly reduce the problem of selecting scaffold branches and the rest of the framework the following winter. And, because this system saves so much of the tree's energy, it can result in a larger tree in a shorter time. Consequently you will get much earlier production.

SELECTION OF SCAFFOLD BRANCHES

Whether you practice summer pruning or leave the whole job until the dormant pruning season, you should give some thought to selection of the scaffold branches. The most desirable tree structure is to start with three scaffold limbs beginning at the trunk. The ideal spacing is limbs six to eight inches apart up and down the trunk and which should be evenly spaced around the trunk. This ideal spacing is seldom possible to achieve, but make as close an approximation to it as possible, taking care to leave the top scaffold branch longer than the others so that it will not be choked out.

During the second summer you can do some additional pruning for the same reason as during the first, in order to eliminate unwanted branches before they make too much growth at the expense of the rest of the tree.

As the tree grows older pruning should be held to a minimum. However, with increasing age more extensive pruning sometimes is needed to maintain the vigor of the tree and allow light to enter. If this is not done the tree will become too dense, shading out the lower part and limiting the bearing area. Water sprouts should be removed, also.

HARVESTING

At maturity the hull of the Almond will split around the suture, either partly or completely depending on variety. As moisture is lost, the hull, shell and kernel will become increasingly dry and the skin of the kernel will turn brown. Cracking will occur first on the nuts on the outside of the tree, gradually working toward the middle. With the drying the nuts become easier to remove and the tendency to fall is increased. But do not harvest until after the nuts in the inner part of the tree have opened.

For easier harvesting the nuts may be knocked down onto sheets or tarps while still slightly green. Hulling, too, is a bit easier if the hull is still moist. Storage of Almond kernels will not be a problem if they are dry and unblanched, and, as with other nuts, they may be put into jars or heavy plastic bags and frozen. I have found that properly handled they will keep almost indefinitely when stored in this manner.

Almonds are a delicious food, good for all-around muscle and body-building. They are good for teeth and bones and especially helpful to the underweight who can use Almond Butter to good advantage. The Almonds' vitamins B[1] and A are particularly good for nursing mothers.

One cup of shelled Almonds (142 grams) contains five percent water, 850 calories of food energy, 26 grams protein, 77 grams fat (total lipid), 28 grams carbohydrate, 332 milligrams calcium, 6.7 milligrams iron, .34 milligrams Thiamine, 1.31 milligrams Riboflavin and 5.0 milligrams Niacin. The nuts also contain unsaturated fatty acids: Oleic 52 grams and Linoleic 15 grams. One pound of Almonds will yield one to one-and-a-half cups of nutmeats.

ALMOND RECIPES

To Blanch Almonds
Cover nuts with cold water. Bring to boiling point and boil for five minutes. Plunge nuts into cold water, drain and rub off skins.

almond milk shake

1 tall glass milk
1 tsp. finely-ground wholewheat
1 tsp. maple syrup
2 tsp. ground Almonds
Mix together all ingredients and chill. This nut milk is a perfectly balanced food drink.

almond butter

Grind or place in blender half cup Almonds, either raw or roasted. Leave the brown skins on.
Mix ground Almonds with cream cheese or mayonnaise.
Or
Add enough oil to finely-ground Almonds to make a paste. Add salt to taste. Refrigerate until ready to use.

salted almonds

½ pound shelled Almonds
2 tablespoons olive oil or melted margarine
salt to taste

Blanch Almonds and dry on paper towels. Place the oil or margarine in a small frying pan and when hot add the Almonds. Saute until evenly and delicately browned. Drain on paper and sprinkle with salt. Cool before serving.

almond-orange bread

2 tablespoons oil
¼ cup sugar
1 egg
2 cups sifted cake flour
3 teaspoons baking powder
1 teaspoon salt
1 cup orange juice
1 teaspoon grated orange rind
1 cup blanched Almonds, coarsely ground

Beat oil, sugar and egg together. Sift flour, baking powder and salt together and add to first mixture alternately with orange juice and rind. Blend thoroughly and add nuts. Pour into oiled loaf pan and bake in moderate oven (350° F.) one hour.

almond-coconut macaroons

¾ cup sugar
¾ cup confectioners sugar
2 tablespoons cake flour
4 egg whites, beaten
2/3 cup ground, blanched Almonds
½ teaspoon vanilla
2¼ cups shredded coconut

Sift together both sugars and flour. Beat egg whites until foamy throughout. Add sugar, 2 tablespoons at a time, beating well after each addition. Fold in Almonds, vanilla and coconut. Drop from teaspoon onto ungreased heavy paper (or teflon-coated cookie sheet). Bake 20 to 25 minutes at 325° F.

almond stuffing for chicken

1 cup soft bread crumbs
½ cup milk
salt and pepper
2 tablespoons margarine, softened
½ cup chopped salted Almonds
Soak crumbs in milk, add remaining ingredients and blend
thoroughly.

10

THE HARDSHELL HICKORIES

Algonkian Indians named this tree family and also taught the early colonists in Virginia to use the ripe nuts of the Shagbark and Mockernut for food. The shells were cracked and the mixture then boiled and strained. The result was a rich, soupy liquid into which they stirred a coarse meal made by grinding Indian corn between two stones.

The mush was cooked slowly until thickened, then made into cakes which were baked on hot stones. Does this sound delicious? It is. Often the soup was eaten alone, and its name "Pocohicora" or "Pohickery" gave the trees their English name. Raffinesque took part of this name, Latinized it, and set it up as the name of the genus.

The Pecan, discussed in a previous chapter, is the best known and most important member of the Hickory family. The others are not as widely planted for nut production, but deserve much more attention, for the flavor of really good Hickory nuts is outstanding and different. In my opinion, even the wild ones are worth digging out of their hard shells.

THE SHAGBARK (CARYA OVATA)

The Shagbark Hickory is well named for it has a gray bark that is shed in thin, tough, vertical strips. Attached by the center, these strips often spring outward at top and bottom, giving the bole a shaggy, untidy look. Young Hickories have smooth bark, this eccentricity occurring only after the trees are older.

In spite of this shaggy look, a Shagbark is a noble tree, expressing strength in every twist of its angular limbs, as the bare oblong of the tree's lofty head is darkly etched against a winter sky. And the durable wood is of an iron hardness that gave Andrew Jackson his nickname "Old Hickory."

The buds of the Shagbark are dark brown and pointed. They have many thin, overlapping scales which persist throughout the winter. The fruits, like those of the Pecan, are encased in four-parted husks, nearly round to oval in shape and varying in size from one-and-a-quarter to one-and-three-quarters inches in diameter. In color the nut is pale, almost white and it has a comparatively thin shell.

THE SHELLBARK (CARYA LACINOSA)

The big Shellbark, like the little Shellbark, is a common forest tree in the Middlewest and middle-Atlantic states. It, too, has a shaggy trunk but the plates are even coarser. In winter the orange-colored twigs, large terminal buds and the persistent stems of the dead leaves are distinguishing traits. In spring the Shellbark Hickory blossom looks as if it should be on a flower stem instead of the branch of a tree.

"King nuts," as the fruits of this tree are called, often are two-and-a-half to three inches long, very impressive looking to hungry nut seekers, and they are of a sweet and delicious flavor. The husks are about a quarter-inch thick, and the shells are light brown in color, hard, thick and bonelike.

Despite their hardness, Hickories have held an immense fascination for small boys for time immemorial. An amusing story is told about a farmer who finally, reaching the limit of his endurance, took down all his signs which read "Posted, Keep Out" and carefully replaced them with "Carya Abound in

These Woods, Enter at Your Own Risk." It is said that for quite some time after that he was not bothered by poaching boys.

MOCKERNUT (CARYA ALBA) AND PIGNUT (C. GLABRA)

As nut-producing trees these two varieties are of little or no importance. The Mockernut, however, does make a beautiful tree and is a most impressive sight in spring when the great buds swell, putting on a surprising show of colors. The outer scales fall and the inner ones expand into rosy, silken sheaths that stand erect around the central cluster of leaves, and every branch seems to be holding up a great, red tulip.

The Pignut is a graceful, symmetrical tree with spreading limbs that end in delicate, pendulous branches. The gray bark is checked into a maze of interesting furrows. The clustered fringes seen in spring among the opening leaves are the green and gold stamen flowers. The fertile flowers, at the tips of the twigs, are green with yellow stigmas and are curiously angled.

The kernels of the Pignut are insipid to taste, but in pioneer days they were of value for fattening pigs which were turned into the forest to forage.

HICANS

Natural hybrids sometimes occur among Hickory species. The most important of these are between *C. lacinosa, C. ovata* (Hickories) and *C. illinoensis* (Pecan), and perhaps a dozen worthwhile varieties have been discovered and named. One of the first named clones (a group of plants all derived by vegetative propagation from one original individual and genetically identical), is the *McCallister*. While this produces a very large and tasty nut it is not abundant, and the tree is mostly of value for shade. This holds true of most of the other hybrids with the exception of the *Burton*, which does produce good crops of quality nuts. Hybridists are hopeful that in time crosses between the northern Shagbark and the northern Pecan may be a means of developing thin-shelled, improved, Hickory varieties for the North.

NAMED VARIETIES OF GRAFTED HICANS

Variety	Size	Flavor
Burton	Medium	Excellent
Underwood	Large	Very good
Clarksville	Large	Good
Pleas Hybrid	Smaller	Good
Gerardi	Large	Very Good
Henke	Medium	Good
McCallister	Extra large	Fair

TO GROW A HICKORY

Because of its extremely long taproot the Hickory is more difficult to transplant than other nut trees. Often it is cut off too short, and since there are very few lateral roots, the tree does not become well established and fails to prosper in its new location.

On the other hand seedling trees are apt to be of small value because of the poor cracking quality of the nuts. Hickory seedlings are more difficult to graft, too, than other nut trees, the availability of good scion wood often being one of the problems.

For these reasons for the farm, homestead or the backyarder who needs only a few trees, the best answer is the nursery-grown tree, which usually has been conditioned for transplanting, making its chances for living good.

Proper planting is of the utmost importance, so make sure that the hole is deep enough to accommodate the root in a vertical position. Fill the hole gradually, firming the soil about the roots as you do. Then see to it that the tree is well watered. Keep the area around the tree free of weeds by cultivation or mulching. I always prefer mulching, which benefits established trees just as much as young ones.

Yard trees can be mulched if you prefer with materials more attractive than rotting leaves. Pine bark, tanbark, ground corncobs or peanut hulls will break down and feed the soil, upon which the tree feeds, with good organic matter. Trees also can be supplied with organic soil matter as a result of fertilizer

Cracking	Bearing	No. of Yrs.
Excellent	Prolific	5-7 Years
Good	Good	5-7 Years
Medium	Good	5-7 Years
Excellent	Good	3-5 Years
Good	Good	3-5 Years
Good	Very good	5-7 Years
Fair	Does not fill well	5-7 Years

application. The peatmoss in the soil mixture that is used to fill fertilizing holes will help keep the soil moist, aerated and well drained.

PRUNING

The pruning of nut trees is aimed primarily at building a strong framework which will support crops of nuts and resist breakage from wind or snow. The principles involved in building a strong tree are the same as for other orchard trees and consist of: (1) avoiding narrow angles between scaffold limbs, (2) avoiding balanced crotches in which the main trunk divides into essentially equal parts, (3) spacing scaffold branches on the trunk so that no two scaffold branches arise at the same level on the trunk.

To accomplish these objectives corrective pruning should be done while the tree is young. Branches forming angles of less than at 45 degrees with the main leader should be removed; one side of a balanced crotch should be cut off or suppressed by pruning it heavily.

As the tree develops, scaffold branches should be chosen that have a vertical distance of 18 to 24 inches between them. If timber logs are wanted later a clean trunk for at least eight feet is sought, and other branches are suppressed or removed.

Weak and strong branch attachments.

Branch with narrow angle attachment may not split until quite large

Long stubs may die back.

Low cut heals over best.

High stub heals over slowly.

Healing wound of correct cut.

Because the growth of a young tree is determined by the amount of leaf surface, pruning should be as light as possible yet helping other objectives sought. Usually it is better to suppress an unwanted branch by pruning it to give permanent branches room, and then to remove it later when the tree attains bearing size. Of course all cuts should be made close to the trunk so that they will heal over. Small pruning cuts heal quickly, but cuts more than an inch in diameter should be treated with antiseptic dressing to prevent entrance of decay or disease while the wound is healing.

POLLINATION

The Hickories have male and female flowers separately on the same shoot of the current season's growth. The staminate (male) catkins, which bear the pollen, occur in clusters at the base of the new shoots. The terminal pistillate (female) flowers with receptive stigmas are at the ends of these same shoots. The pollen, which is windborne, is produced and shed abundantly at about the same time the leaves are fully expanded.

HARVESTING

Hickories like Pecans are encased in four-parted husks from which they drop. Rake or gather them into piles and do this often, for Hickories are notoriously attractive to squirrels which know a good thing when they see it. Store the nuts at room temperature in any cool, dry place and they will keep for months. The hard shells will never get any softer, but I have found that a hot water bath will make the shelling task easier. I soak them for 10 to 15 minutes. If the shells are especially hard you may even try boiling. You will derive about one pound of nutmeats (or about four cups) from three pounds of nuts in the shell.

HICKORY RECIPES

hickory nut drops

1/3 cup cooking oil
1 cup brown sugar
2 eggs
2 cups cake flour
2 teaspoons baking powder
½ cup milk
1½ teaspoon vanilla
1 cup Hickory nuts,
    chopped or coarsely ground

Cream oil and sugar together until fluffy. Add eggs one at a time
beating thoroughly. Sift flour and baking powder together and
add alternately with milk to creamed mixture. Fold in vanilla
and nuts. Drop from teaspoon onto oiled cookie sheet and bake
15 minutes at 375° F.

From my friends among the Cherokee I have the two following
recipes:

hickory nut pie

½ cup butter or margarine
3 eggs slightly beaten
½ teaspoon salt
1½ cups chopped Hickory nuts
1 cup sugar
¾ cup dark corn syrup
1½ teaspoons vanilla

Combine ingredients and bake in an unbaked pie shell 15
minutes at 450° F. Reduce heat to 350° F. and continue baking
until well done — about 35 to 40 minutes.

conutchia (hickory nuts)

1 cup hominy grits
1½ cups Hickory nuts
Cook hominy grits until tender. Beat Hickory nuts to a fine
pulp (hulls and all) until the mass can be pressed together to
form a ball. When hominy grits are done put the nuts in a
pan and cover with boiling water. Use enough water to stir nuts
well to remove hulls, then strain through a fine sieve to catch
any remaining. Add to hominy grits and serve with sugar or salt.

Here is a more sophisticated version of:

hickory and hominy casserole

1 10½ ounce can condensed cream
    of mushroom soup
½ cup coffee cream
¼ teaspoon cayenne
1½ teaspoon Worcestershire
    sauce
1 teaspoon celery salt
½ teaspoon pepper
1 No. 2½ can hominy
½ pound Hickory nuts
    chopped
1 cup buttered whole-
    wheat crumbs
Mix mushroom soup, cream, cayenne, Worcestershire sauce,
celery salt and pepper. Simmer over low fire until well blended.
Preheat oven to 350° F. Drain hominy, place in oiled casserole.
Add Hickory nuts to soup mixture. Pour over hominy. Cover
with buttered crumbs. Bake approximately ½ hour.

golden cheese salad

3 ounce package lemon-
    flavored gelatin
1 cup boiling water
1 cup pineapple juice
1½ ounces cream cheese
1/3 cup Hickory nuts
10½ ounce can crushed
    pineapple, drained
1 cup carrots, shredded
Lettuce leaves, if desired

Dissolve gelatin in boiling water. Stir in pineapple juice. Chill until partially set. Cut cream cheese into 18 cubes. Coat cream cheese cubes with nuts and roll into balls. Stir pineapple and carrots into gelatin. Add cream cheese balls. Chill several hours or overnight until firm. Serve on lettuce leaves.

nippy cheese nut dip

2 packages (3 oz. each)
    softened cream cheese
¼ cup mayonnaise
¼ teaspoon onion salt
¼ teaspoon Hickory salt
⅛ teaspoon garlic salt
    (or to taste)
½ cup toasted Hickory nuts,
    chopped

Blend cream cheese with mayonnaise and seasonings. Stir in nuts. Good to serve with potato chips or crackers.

fruit and nut sauce

10 oz. package sweetened
    frozen fruit (strawberries,
    red raspberries, or mixed
    fruit) thawed and drained.
1 cup liquid from frozen fruit
    plus water
¼ cup sugar
1 tablespoon cornstarch
1 tablespoon raisins, chopped
2 tablespoons lemon juice
¼ teaspoon rum extract
¼ cup Hickory nuts, toasted
    and chopped

Cut large pieces of fruit into bite-sized pieces. Stir fruit liquid gradually into sugar, cornstarch and raisins in a saucepan. Cook over medium heat, stirring constantly, until clear and thickened. Add lemon juice, rum extract, Hickory nuts and fruit. May be served over ice cream or warm cake.

11

THE VERSATILE PEANUT

Peanuts are one nut crop you don't have to wait for, and what's more they will grow just about anywhere that suitable soil conditions permit. The big, sweet *Tennessee Reds* (Parks) will grow as far north as New York, and the small, delicious *Early Spanish* (Stokes) even will grow and mature a crop in Canada!

Peanuts are truly an all-American nut, and they discovered the Americas long before Columbus set foot in the New World, probably growing first in Peru, where pottery jars shaped like Peanuts and other artifacts with Peanut designs were found in Inca tombs. Similar items found in Bolivia and northeastern Argentina show that Peanuts were grown and treasured there also.

The Spanish Conquistadors coming to South America for gold didn't realize at the time that they had something even better in Peanuts. Nevertheless, they were taken back to Spain where they became an important crop of that country.

Spanish ships took Peanuts to Africa, too, where they were traded for spices and elephant tusks and were called "Goobers" by the Africans. During the 18th century slave traders enroute to America bought the cheapest and all unknowingly the best food available in Africe — Peanuts.

The Peanut has enjoyed a remarkable rise in popularity and importance in the last century. During the War Between the States, Union and Confederate soldiers alike came to appreciate the Peanut for its taste, food energy and nourishment, ease in preparation and keeping qualities. Soldiers returned from the battlefields to their scattered homes with a taste for Peanuts — and in some instances a pocketful to back up their praise.

The number of people engaged in the Peanut industry has steadily grown to the present day when the annual U.S. crop, widely planted and voraciously consumed, is three billion pounds, and has a farm value of over $385,000,000.

Dr. George Washington Carver contributed greatly to the usefulness, profitability and popularity of Peanuts. He discovered that Peanuts are rich in protein, fats and other body-building elements and developed over 300 uses for them. His ingenuity led to the discovery of ways and means to use every part of the Peanut plant.

Peanuts, both the nutmeat, the shell and the plant, are used in many diversified ways in industry. Food products include milk, flour, Peanut butter, margarine, cooking and salad oil, cheese, mayonnaise, confections, meal, candies. Non-food products include shaving cream, adhesives, paper, ink, plastics, salve, cosmetics, shampoo, shoe polish, dyes, lubricating oils, metal polish, fertilizer, fodder for livestock, insulation filler, buffing for steel mills, floor sweeping compound, wallboard and carrier for certain deactivated chemicals.

Botanically Peanuts may be divided into three main types — the Virginia, Spanish, and Runner — based on the branching order and pattern and the number of seeds per pod. The seeds usually are two for the Virginia, two to three for the Spanish type, and three or four for the Runner. The Valencia may have three to six seeds per pod.

The Peanut is distinguished by its yellow, papilionaceous (resembling a butterfly) flowers which are borne above ground. Following fertilization, (usually by bee pollinators), the flower wilts, and after a period of five to seven days a geotropic (curving earthward) peg or ovary emerges. It requires 145 to 150 days for the Peanut to mature, but the Early Spanish will make in 100 to 120 days.

1. Blossom cut length-
wise
2. Ripe nut
3. Nut cut lengthwise
4. Seed
5 & 6. Germ

HOW TO GROW PEANUTS

Arachis hypogaea L. (Peanut) leads an unusual growth and production life. The Spanish type grows in clusters near the taproot of the plant, and it prefers a light and sandy soil along with a warm climate. In the Northern states and in Canada it is advisable to plant by May 15th to June 1st to ensure enough time for the Peanuts to form.

The nutlike seed is concealed in every Peanut resting snugly between two meaty halves as the embryo. The whole nut is planted and the two halves (cotyledons) provide rich stores of food for the young plant until it is established in the soil.

In spite of their name, Peanuts are no more nuts than the Almond. They actually are legumes and justly can be called a Ground Pea, since they belong to the pea and bean family.

Peanuts rank high in six nutritional categories: food energy, protein, fats, niacin, thiamine, and phosphorous, while their poly-unsaturated fatty acids make them valuable as energy foods. In addition they furnish appreciable amounts of calcium, iron, copper, and magnesium.

Each Peanut flower is complete, containing both male (anther) and female (stigma) for reproduction. And, because both parts are enclosed in the flower, self-fertilization generally occurs rather than cross-fertilization.

When fertilized, the ovary begins to enlarge and extend to form a "peg" which gravity pulls toward the soil. This peg carries the newly-formed embryo at its tip. After penetrating the soil two to seven centimeters it turns sideways and the pod begins to form.

Plant your Peanuts about two inches deep in rows 24 to 36 inches apart. Drop the seeds about four to six inches apart in the row. Pack the soil down firmly for good contact. You may do this with the flat of a hoe or by walking over each row as you finish planting. Shelled Peanuts also may be planted, but break the shells with care so as not to break or disturb the pink, papery covering of the nuts.

In growing conditions of warmth, air and moisture, a complex set of growth-control enzymes begins to take over within the embryo now snugly resting in the earth. Certain cells begin to enlarge causing the seed to swell.

When soil temperature reaches somewhere between 65 and 70° the seed germinates. If conditions are right this will happen about two days after planting and the tip of the primary root will break through the seed coat and start downward. Approximately five days after planting the primary root is already about six inches long and lateral roots are appearing.

While this is happening a peculiar white structure (hypocotyl), located just above the true roots, starts to enlarge. This pushes the two halves of the seed coat (cotyledons) upward. The emerging shoots will crack the soil surface about eight days after planting.

Progress is steady, and in about 14 days the first "square" of four leaves will unfold, each leaf consisting of a slender stem (petiole), bearing four leaflets. Look at the crown of the plant and you will see a cluster of leaflets, still folded, from which new shoot growth will continue to emerge.

Just above the attachment of each cotyledon, lateral branches start developing and these lower laterals are the primary origin of flowering branches which will develop later. In early cultivation you must be careful to avoid injuring or burying them.

After about eight to 12 weeks all the pegs that will develop into mature pods have entered the soil and enlargement has begun to take place. Of course the yield and quality of the kernels in the pods determines the value of the crop. The plant will continue to grow and flower as the season progresses and eventually will produce some 40 or more mature pods.

With the approach of maturity the plants start to lose some of their rich green color because the kernels are using the plant's food supply for their own growth.

Eventually the point is reached where the full-mature pods just barely make up for the shedding of the overmature pods. This is the time to begin harvesting.

Planters in northern sections who have put in the *Early Spanish* will be able to start harvesting the smaller nuts sooner, for it requires only about 120 days for these to mature. But, as fall approaches, digging expands to all sections and by the last of September or October is virtually complete.

NUTRITIVE VALUE OF SALTED PEANUTS (3/4 OUNCE)

Protein grams	Energy calories	Fat Grams	Calcium milligrams	Phosphorus milligrams
5.57	125	10.7	.16	.86

Iron milligrams	Niacin milligrams	Riboflavin milligrams	Thiamine milligrams
.45	3.7	.028	.068

DIG PEANUTS CAREFULLY

To save as many Peanuts as possible there are several points to consider. The condition of the soil is important, it must be neither too wet nor too dry. The preferred soil for peanuts is a sandy loam, which is conductive to their best growth and also makes them easier to harvest. The pods should be lifted gently without pulling them off the vines or permitting them to stick in wet soil. A digger is your best tool — one with a long blade that runs three to four inches under the soil — for loosening the plant and cutting the taproot.

When this is done by machine, a shaker comes along immediately behind the blade, lifts the Peanuts from the soil and gently shakes them and lifts onto the rear of the digger-shaker. The small grower will need to do this by hand.

Leave your Peanuts "fluffy" in the windrow and curing will take place rapidly. In most parts of the Southeast and Southwest the Peanuts are allowed to remain in the windrow until the moisture content is eight to 10 percent — usually about a week to ten days in favorable weather. In climates farther north complete field curing may be impossible and large plantings are cured by using heat and forced air to complete the process. Hanging or stacking the Peanuts loosely in a warm, airy room will work well for the small planter.

SOIL REQUIREMENTS FOR PEANUTS

Peanuts do best on well drained sandy and sandy loam soils with friable, sandy or sandy clay subsoils. The pegs can penetrate readily and the crop usually can be harvested without soil clinging to the nuts. The plants also can be plowed out with very few Peanuts remaining in the ground.

Fine textured soils, such as clay loams and clays, may produce good yields when moisture conditions are favorable, but they often form crusts which the pegs cannot penetrate readily to set a crop. Then harvesting may be difficult, for many of the pegs will break off and leave nuts in the ground. Dark colored soils will discolor the hulls, and in clay particles may cling to the nuts. For the home grower this is not great disaster, but for the commercial grower the grade will be lowered.

MAINTAINING SOIL FERTILITY

Peanuts as members of the legume family take nitrogen from the air, but the manner in which the crop is harvested and utilized creates a soil condition which requires careful management. The sandy soils used may be deficient in organic matter, nitrogen, phosphorus and potassium, which must be replaced as successive crops are planted. In home gardens it is a good idea to rotate the space where Peanuts are grown from year to year. I like to grow them as a second crop after an early one has been harvested.

IRRIGATION

Peanuts respond well to irrigation, and if natural rainfall is slight watering usually will be necessary. Before planting time it's a good idea to check the amount of moisture in the soil to a depth of about three feet. If the soil moisture is adequate at planting time the first watering usually can be put off until the plants start blooming, but moisture is critical in the period of blooming and nut development. Do *not* apply water too near to harvest time as this will result in immature nuts and excessive moisture in the mature ones. It even may start the mature nuts under the main body of the plant into growth, and they will be ruined.

LIMESTONE AND GYPSUM

When Peanuts are grown on soils that are very low in available calcium, an application of either limestone or gypsum (calcium sulfate) may increase the yield and improve the nut quality. Calcium deficiency has very little effect on the vegetative growth of the Peanut plants but there will be many unfilled pods.

CULTIVATION AND HARVEST

Start weed control as soon as the plants are up, but be careful not to cultivate too close to the plants. Hand pull a few weeds if you must.

I like to harvest Peanuts in our home garden when the leaves begin to turn yellow and the kernels are fully developed. At this time the veins inside the pods will begin to darken in color. At the same time the Peanut skins will be light pink and papery thin.

At digging time I check a plant or two from different parts of the rows, and then dig when at least 80 percent of the Peanuts are mature, especially when the pods immediately under the *main plant* are ready. This is the most important part of your harvest especially in northern areas. The crop grown on the pegs seldom matures, and if you wait for it you will only delay the harvest beyond the time when the mature nuts under the plant should be taken.

Remember, too, after you have removed the nuts that the vines also are valuable. Turn them under in the garden or place them on your compost pile. Years ago when we kept milk goats we always saved the Peanut hay as the biggest treat for them from our fall garden.

TO CARE FOR YOUR PEANUTS

The principal factor causing spoilage of Peanuts is their high content of fat, which becomes rancid easily in improper storage, particularly when the Peanuts are shelled. To retain crispness and flavor they should be stored in tightly-closed containers and refrigerated. Peanuts in the shell keep better than shelled nuts, which keep better if not salted.

PEANUT RECIPES

These are basic rules upon which many Peanut recipes are based. All are easy.

blanching

To blanch shelled, raw Peanuts put them into boiling water and let stand 3 minutes. Drain. Slide skins off with your fingers. Spread nuts on absorbent paper to dry.

Roasting will also loosen the skins of Peanuts either shelled or unshelled.

french frying

Using a good vegetable oil, preferably Peanut oil, cook raw, blanched Peanuts in deep oil with wire basket or shallow oil with no basket. Oil must be deep enough to cover Peanuts. Heat oil to 300° F., add Peanuts. Stir occasionally to assure even cooking. When Peanuts begin browning, remove from oil as they will continue to brown while cooling. Drain Peanuts and spread on brown paper (bags from the grocery will do), for further draining. Salt immediately according to taste, using fine-ground popcorn salt for best results.

roasting shelled peanuts

Place raw blanched shelled Peanuts one layer deep in shallow baking pan. Roast 350° F. for 15 to 20 minutes until golden brown. Stir occasionally for even roasting. Coat with melted margarine, then salt to taste.

roasting peanuts in the shell

Place Peanuts one or two layers deep in shallow baking pan. Roast at 350° F. for 25 to 30 minutes, stirring occasionally. Shell and sample the Peanuts during the last few minutes of cooking time to assure they are roasted to the desired doneness.

glazed peanuts

1 cup sugar
½ cup water
2 cups raw, shelled,
    unblanched Peanuts

Dissolve sugar in water in a heavy frying pan over medium heat. Add Peanuts and continue cooking on medium high heat, stirring constantly. Cook until the Peanuts have a shiny, glazed, rosy look. Spread onto aluminum foil to cool. Break apart while still warm. After cooling, store in airtight container.

peanut butter

1 cup salted, roasted
   Spanish Peanuts
1 tablespoon Peanut oil
½ teaspoon salt
honey (optional)

Place ingredients in an electric blender. Blend until mixture becomes paste-like or spreadable. It may be necessary to add more Peanut oil. The ingredients must be blended for several minutes. Store in tightly-covered container. Homemade Peanut butter will separate on standing. Stir before using. A teaspoon or two of Honey may be added after blending. Make your Peanut butter in small quantities and store any not used in your refrigerator. Peanut butter hardens with cold so remove and let stand a short time when you wish to use it again.

peanut butter shake

4 cups milk
4 tablespoons Carob powder (Carob has
   the taste of chocolate and great
   nutritional qualities)
½ cup maple syrup
1/3 cup creamy Peanut butter
2 cups (1 pint) vanilla ice cream

Note: Carob, unlike tea, coffee and chocolate does not contain oxalic acid.

Combine all ingredients in large bowl and beat together, or place in blender. Makes 6 tall glasses.

baked peanut butter chicken

2½ to 3 pound frying
   chicken, cut up
¼ cup flour
1 egg
1/3 cup Peanut butter
   (smooth or crunchy)
1 teaspoon salt
⅛ teaspoon pepper
1/3 cup milk
½ cup dry bread crumbs
¼ cup Peanut oil

Dip chicken in flour. Blend egg with Peanut butter, salt and
pepper. Gradually add milk, beating with fork to blend. Dip
floured chicken in Peanut butter mixture then in crumbs. Place
on oiled flat baking pan. Dribble remaining oil over chicken
pieces. Bake in oven (375° F.) 45 minutes or until tender.

peanut butter meat balls

½ cup Peanut butter
   (smooth or crunchy)
½ pound ground beef
¼ cup finely chopped onion
2 tablespoons chili sauce
1 teaspoon salt
⅛ teaspoon pepper
1 egg beaten
2 tablespoons Peanut oil
2 cups seasoned tomato sauce

Mix Peanut butter lightly with beef, onion, chili sauce, salt,
pepper and egg. Form into 12 meatballs. Brown in hot Peanut
oil. Add tomato sauce, cover and simmer 30 minutes. Serve with
cooked rice or spaghetti.

ham puffs

1 egg, separated
½ cup Peanut butter
½ cup ground ham
1 teaspoon grated onion
¼ teaspoon salt
30 crisp, round crackers
Combine beaten egg yolk, Peanut butter, ham, onion and salt; fold into stiffly beaten egg white. Place small spoonfuls of mixture on each cracker. Place on baking sheet. Bake at 350° F. for 30 minutes. Serve hot.

Note: A 30-page booklet of Peanut recipes may be obtained from the Oklahoma Peanut Commission, Box D, Madill, Oklahoma 73446.

12

PINYON NUT TREES

I have frequently feasted on the Southwest's delicious Pinyon nut and have come to hold it in high regard. The two-needled Pinyon, *Pinus edulis*, a shaggy evergreen tree, produces a food nut which was used by the aborigines in the Southwest. It was a staple the year around, and was second only to maize. The basket makers, who preceded the cliff dwellers, harvested and stored the nuts, too. There are dozens of stories of Indians and others who, lost and beset by storms, have survived in the mountains because they knew enough to hunt for and rob the nests of ground squirrels and pack rats.

It was not until the early 1920's that Pinyon nuts became a cash crop. At that time machines were invented to hull the nuts and soon they were packaged, marketed and sold from coast to coast. The natural nuts are oily, sweet, nutritious and delicious. Pinyons can be used in many ways the Peanut is — toasted and salted or in candy and pastry. The Indians of the deep southwest have more than fifty ways or preparing tasty Pinyon dishes, ranging from an appetizing additive to stews and gruels to the sweetest of cakes and cookies.

Before grinding into flour the Pinyons are washed two or three times, removing the last speck of rusty-brown dust from the hulls. Next they are boiled and then roasted. The roasted nuts are ground, hull and all, on a *metate* (grinding stones) just as they were centuries ago. Roasting makes the hulls very brittle by removing the gum and oil, and it also improves the flavor.

The process is much the same as for grinding corn. First the nuts are roughly cracked and broken up, hulls and kernels together. The second grinding turns this into a very fine flour, the quality depending upon how thoroughly the oil has been removed in the roasting process.

After the second grinding the flour is allowed to dry further, and the natural evaporation of any remaining oil leaves it crusty. A third grinding follows, and then it is ready to use.

Most often the flour is sweetened a bit with sugar or syrup, and then is placed in a pan and baked slowly over a bed of coals. The hot cake is kept carefully just under the temperature where any remaining oil would fry away. If the Pinyons are freshly gathered the oil gives them a tastier flavor. The cakes cook quickly and are removed and allowed to cool. They may be cut with a knife or easily broken into tasty chunks-very tempting to children who love Pinyon bread. I like it too.

Another favorite among the Navajos is Pinyon nut mush which is rather like corn meal mush in appearance. The nuts are not ground but are hulled and broken into coarse chunks, which then are boiled, drained and allowed to set. When firm it is fried like scrapple but becomes a kind of waffle. This can be folded together while it is still warm and pliable, and as it dries, the light pieces can be broken off and eaten that way.

The Pinyon *(P. edulis)* ranges from the eastern foothills of the Colorado Rockies to western Texas and westward to the eastern border of Utah, southwestern Wyoming, central Arizona and on into Mexico. It often forms extensive open forests and will grow to elevations of seven thousand feet. The short and stiff needle leaves in clusters of two or three, are dark green, ridged and stout, and may persist for eight or nine years.

The tree is a broad, compact pyramid as it ages, becoming dense and round-topped with stout branches which produce abundant globose cones. Each scale covers two seeds, wingless and about the size of honey locust seeds.

Other Pinyon pines that produce nuts are *P. quadrifolia,* which is scattered over the mountains of southern and Lower California; *P. cembroides,* which covers the upper slopes of the

Arizona mountains, and *P. monophylla*. This latter Pinyon has abundant fruit which are short, oblong and about two inches in length. The Indians of Nevada and California have long depended upon them for food.

Pinyon trees require two years to produce a crop, the embryo cone coming from a flowering bud which matures the following year. There is a widely held belief that a tree produces nuts only in odd-numbered years — the third, fifth or seventh. This is not true, though in the arid Southwest several years may elapse before conditions are favorable for a stand of trees to "put on." Pinyon pines bear according to the amount of moisture available, particularly as related to the past winter's snow. Because of this trees in some areas may not produce nuts for three, four years or longer. But when water is plentiful during winter and early spring, even a tree bearing maturing cones will blossom and bud. And another crop then can be harvested from the same tree the following year.

The cones, from embryo to mature size, are dark green and thickly covered with pitch which protects the growing nuts from insects that might bore into them. Indians use the gum for water-proofing objects such as water jars of woven willow, also use it as a skin salve, and burned into chunks as herb dyes.

Many consider the Pinyon tree a weather prognosticator. Indians will tell you that when it blossoms in the spring there will be a stormy, snowy winter followed by a wet spring. Otherwise, they believe, the tree would not put on. When it does blossom they believe it is an indication of a fine growing season, and they plant their field crops accordingly, even in the most arid regions.

Pinyon pines usually grow 10 to 20 feet in height. The densely branched *P. cembroides* is hardy only in mild climates but its varieties, *edulis* and *monophylla*, may be grown as far north as Massachusetts. The trees are very picturesque, attractive and bushy when young and have rounded tops in old age, the leaves borne in pairs and the young growth intensely blue. They are obtainable from Mellinger's, Inc., North Lima, Ohio, and the plants come potted.

Pinyons should be set in their permanent places when quite small, since they tend to form long, straggly roots which are not easy to dig with a good soil ball about them. Yet to do this is important to the successful transplanting of all except very small specimens.

Planting time is early fall or in spring, just before new

growth begins. Dig your holes one-and-a-half to two feet deep and at least a foot wider all around than the root ball. When the holes are dug, the topsoil is kept aside and separate from the subsoil. After the transplanted tree is set in position in the hole, this topsoil should be packed around the roots. If the location is an exposed one, plant with the heads of the trees leaning a little into the wind. If there is any danger before they have become well rooted of wind loosening the trees at the collar (the point where the trunk joins the mass of roots at about ground level), they should be staked or supported by guy wires.

Most Pinyons give best results when planted on dry or well-drained land. It's a waste of time to plant them where the ground is waterlogged or sour. They do not require rich soil, but grow well in good loam, and may even grow luxuriantly on sand and sandy peat.

How you prune (or don't) your Pinyon pines depends on how you grow them. Those grown under forest conditions need little pruning, but ornamental trees require more careful handling. There is a general tendency among pines to produce large branches low down on the stem, and if these are not removed they will take the food material that should go to build up the trunk.

You must decide and act accordingly whether you want to produce bushy trees, branched to the ground line, or trees that will appear with a definite length of trunk clear of branches. If you do not want to clear the trunk there is no need for regular pruning. If you *do* want to clear it, you must begin by removing the lower branches while the trees are very young.

When removing branches from vigorous young pines, do not cut them quite back to the bark of the trunk but to a slight swelling that appears around the base of the branch. If this swollen part is left the wound will cover quickly with new wood. This is one of the few cases where a close cut is not the best one. Dead and poorly placed branches should be removed from older trees.

Pine nuts have been used as food for centuries, not only by the Indians of the Southwest but in many parts of Asia, Europe and the Middle East as well as in South America. They differ a little in color, shape, size and flavor depending on where they are found, but are essentially the same.

The Korean pine is considered an excellent choice to plant in even the smallest of gardens, both as an ornamental evergreen and for the harvest of nuts. The tree is slow-growing and develops a pyramidial form with dense foliage. It is very hardy and will produce large numbers of cones containing edible seeds of fine flavor. The nuts have tight, thin but hard shells with kernels as large as Spanish peanuts. They are hardy enough to grow up into Zone 3.

Pine nuts combine well with all kinds of meats such as chicken, turkey, ham, pork, veal, mutton or lamb. They make excellent stuffings and sauces for duck and game birds, and they also are good with vegetables, rice or fish. While they are fine "as is" for certain dishes, I think the flavor is improved by toasting.

To do this spread the nuts in a single layer on an unoiled baking sheet. Preheat oven to 350° F. and toast until just golden brown, stirring often so they will brown evenly. They burn quickly, so watch closely.

Pine nuts are good keepers. Stored in a covered container at room temperature they will remain good for many months, and placed in the refrigerator they will keep even longer.

PINYON RECIPES
chicken with pine nuts

1 tablespoon butter or margarine
1 tablespoon onion, finely chopped
½ cup celery, chopped
10 ounce package green beans, frozen
    French-style
1 tablespoon pimiento, chopped
2 cups chicken, cooked, diced
2 cans, 10½ ounces each,
    cream of mushroom soup
½ teaspoon oregano
⅛ teaspoon white pepper
2/3 cup Pinyon nuts
1 tablespoon parsley, minced

Melt fat in two- or three-quart saucepan. Add onion, celery and beans. Cover and simmer over low heat about 15 minutes, stirring occasionally, until beans are tender. Add pimiento, chicken, soup and seasonings. Cook 10 minutes longer to blend flavors, stirring as needed to prevent sticking. Stir in nuts. Sprinkle with parsley before serving.

pine nuts with tuna (a variation)

Omit fat and chicken. Cook onion, celery and beans in half cup water instead of fat. Use a 13-ounce can of water-pack tuna, drained, in place of chicken. Continue as for recipe with chicken.

chicken-pine nuts-tomato cups

Add one-half cup Pine nuts to chicken salad just before serving. Core six tomatoes; cut into wedges partially through each tomato. Top tomatoes with salad.

waldorf date-nut

Add one-half cup pitted chopped dates to a tart Waldorf salad. Gently stir in one-half cup Pine nuts. Serve immediately.

13

SPECIAL NUT INFORMATION

If you have acquired woodland quite likely it will be mixed stand having trees of all sizes — from seed-producing mature trees with a good volume of wood to small seedlings.

If property comes to you by inheritance you take what's there, but if you are buying remember that for good cash return your forest must be where the climate and soil can grow paying trees. For this the land must be fairly level so that it is possible to get to the trees to harvest the crop and haul them out without going to too much expense.

An acre of hardwood trees may be expected to grow about a cord of new wood a year, and if you cut more than this you will decrease the capital asset of that acre.

Trees such as gray birch, chokecherry and scrub oak are considered weed trees, and thinning them out will encourage your more valuable trees to grow. This also reduces crowding and the shading of seedlings, which need sunlight to grow to replace those that are cut. Thinnings need not be wasted, can be utilized for fuel, fence posts and bean poles to name a few uses.

Trees to be selectively cut always should be well marked in

advance. Don't choose and cut at the same time. Mark the trees plainly with a paint brush or hand-spray gun and at a time when you are not hurried to make a quick decision.

Pecan, Walnut and Hickory are slower-growing trees than poplar and sweet gum, for instance. If your nut trees are giving you a good harvest you probably will want to keep as many as possible as long as possible. However, even these trees grow larger in time and begin to crowd each other. That is when you must choose with even greater care, balancing the value of the nuts against the value of the timber. Of course you will keep the best producers if a choice is possible.

Salable timber standing in a forest before trees are felled is called "stumpage" and the price is based on the purchaser of the trees doing the felling and hauling. The trees may go to three different kinds of markets: for fuel wood, pulp or saw logs.

The wood of nut trees is particularly valuable for veneer and at present Walnut, either Black or English, is one of the most preferred kinds. Butternut, Hickory and Pecan as well as lesser-known nut trees can supply wood on a commercial basis, or perhaps just enough for a home project such as paneling or crafting furniture.

14

FOIL THOSE PREDATORS

RABBITS

Rabbits can do serious damage to young nut trees at any time of the year, but they are particularly apt to cause problems in winter when food is scarce.

Probably the best way to insure complete protection is the use of galvanized hardware cloth or one- to two-inch mesh chicken wire. A guard of quarter-inch mesh hardware cloth placed around young nut trees also will protect against mice. It will last for many years, so be sure to allow sufficient room for several years growth of the tree trunk.

Such a circle of cloth or wire should be about 18 inches high and imbedded in the soil at the tree base at least four and preferably six inches. Tar paper cylinders tied around young trees also will give protection from rabbits.

Many authorities say to pull mulch away from the base of the tree to expose bare soil during the fall and winter. I feel that with the wire or tar paper to protect the trunk from girdling, a mulch can remain and be very helpful. Alternate freezing and thawing

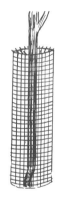

Set hardware cloth 4 to 6 inches below the surface.

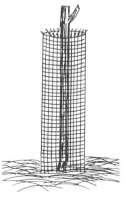

Place mulch outside hardware cloth.

of the bare soil can loosen the roots of young trees, sometimes partially heaving them out of the ground.

Rabbit repellents often used include dried blood, which many consider effective and also is good for the garden soil. Others paint the tree trunks in the fall with fat. Rabbits will not touch this material since they are vegetarians, but it may attract rodents.

A good commercial rabbit repellent is "Rabbit Rid" (Henry Field), which is effective for up to two months and then must be renewed. In winter it will keep rabbits away from small trees at the snow line.

Sometimes prunings left on the ground around the trees will feed the rabbits enough to keep them from injuring the trunks. Plants of the onion family are known to repel them, so you might try planting it in a circle around your trees. They're good at any time to repel borers.

Another device I have seen used is cutting up an old garden hose into three- or four-foot lengths and placing them in strategic areas, coiled a bit to look like snakes.

SQUIRRELS

There's no getting around the fact that squirrels love nuts, and they are going to harvest all they can from your trees if you give them half a chance. Where I live we have cute little red squirrels, and I see them running, jumping and climbing all over town, especially during the fall and winter months when they come in from the country.

An isolated tree is fairly easy to protect with a squirrel guard made of slippery smooth metal which encircles the trunk in the form of a downward cone. Make sure that it is wide enough so the squirrels cannot climb over it.

Another possibility is the use of a smooth aluminum or heavy plastic band too wide for the squirrels to cross. This shield should allow for expansion of the tree trunk by means of two holes and slots for the spikes. Bands of viscous materials, such as tree tanglefoot used for tree banding against insects, may be effective, too.

Tree band of aluminum has slots to allow for expansion as the tree grows. Smooth metal encircles trunk downward in a cone.

Sometimes it is possible to repel tree squirrels by placing mothballs at the base of trees, or nylon net bags filled with mothballs hung in trees. Red squirrels, like rabbits, dislike onions. If not too numerous sometimes squirrels can be live trapped and transported away from the area.

BIRDS

Where birds are few in number they present no real problem, but large flocks roosting in the trees may be detrimental as well as a nuisance. Noise-makers such as tin cans containing glass marbles often are used to frighten birds away. Carbide cannons or exploders set to fire at certain intervals sound like a blast from a shotgun. These may work in small orchards where other devices are ineffective.

A bird tanglefoot (Henry Field) now available, and which is non-poisonous, odorless and will not injure birds, repels them because they dislike the sticky substance on their feet. One application will give control for a year.

Sometimes a farmer will hang a few dead crows in his trees to frighten others away. Two other plans seem to work well for us! One is to use discarded half or gallon size milk cartons suspended from the tree branches in such a way that they are in almost perpetual motion. The other idea is to take lengths of garden hose and hang them in the trees to simulate snakes. The hose can be made to look even more realistic if brightly colored tape is banded on the "snake" in a pattern of diamonds or stripes. You may even cut a slit in one side of a rubber ball, insert one end of the hose, and paint eyes on the ball to resemble those of a snake. A large hairpin makes an effective forked "tongue."

Birds respond differently to scaring devices, and what will work with one may not be effective with another. Simple effigies that remain still usually are less effective than moving ones. Moving ones combined with noise are still better.

No matter what technique you decide on begin early in the season. Once birds have become accustomed to roosting in trees or feeding on them it is very difficult to change their habits. You

Milk Whirlers, From Top to Bottom:
Wash half or gallon carton, reseal top. Slit carton on all four sides, top to bottom. Cut fishline desired length. Cut in half and attach sections of bead chain to act as swivel. Squash carton. Wind enters openings and causes it to whirl. Attach line to carton.

may find it helpful to try different approaches on alternate days. The element of surprise has value and even timing makes a difference. Noisemakers used at daybreak, during the first hours of bird activity, will be more likely to keep them away. Once they have settled down and started to feed they are likely to remain the rest of the day.

RATS AND MICE

Rats usually do not prove to be a problem in a nut orchard, but I remember one year when apparently there was a rat population explosion all over the United States. Rats usually hide in the daytime, but that year the starving creatures would come out of their hiding places and gather Pecans with me in the orchard. I have never known this to happen before or since.

Mice, however, often cause serious damage both to nuts and seedlings. Nuts that are to be buried for planting in the spring should always be protected by ¼-inch mesh hardware cloth. As with rabbits, tar paper (black felt roofing paper) wrapped around the trunks of young trees will repel mice, possibly because of the creosote and asphalt tars in the paper. Both rats and mice are repelled by pitch pine and camphor as well as the fresh or dried leaves of mints and their oils.

Mulch around young trees often provides hiding places for rodents during the winter, but the hardware cloth that guards against rabbits also will keep them away. Mowing older orchards during the growing season, which removes both food and cover and exposes the mice to their natural enemies, is an effective extra control.

DEER

Browsing deer also may seriously damage young seedlings. This usually happens during the winter, but may also occur during the growing season. Since deer are high jumpers any protective fence needs to be eight feet or more tall to be effective. Commercial repellents such as "Deerban" are partially successful, but after two months they must be renewed. They are used during budding time as well as during the winter.

MOLES

If you live in a area where moles are prevalent and you decide to grow Peanuts, they may give you some problems. I don't know whether they actually eat the Peanut seeds or not — I suspect they do — but you may be sure the Peanuts will not come up if moles tunnel under the row before they sprout. Once the Peanuts are up and growing the moles seldom seem to bother them.

There are a number of ways to repel moles, some as simple as using noise-makers, since moles seem to detest noise. Some people get good results by placing empty bottles in the runs or children's toy pinwheels at strategic intervals. There are commercial baits, too, such as "Mole-Nots," or a row of castor bean plants planted around the garden is believed to protect against moles which apparently dislike the roots. Mole traps are another solution.

If animals of any kind must be trapped — and sometimes this is the only way to protect crops — I strongly recommend that you use the Havahart small animal trap which will catch raiding rabbits and squirrels as well as pigeons and sparrows but does them no injury. Pets or poultry captured by accident can be released unharmed.

CONCLUSION

So let's stop treating nuts like culinary stepchildren and put them back where they belong in the main course dishes, in soups and salads, in meat loaves, with vegetables, rice, potatoes or pasta. They deserve better than just use for snacks and desserts, delightful as they are this way. The housewife of yesteryear used nuts in all her favorite dishes, taking them for granted and keeping them on hand ready to be added anytime she felt like it. Nuts were as commonplace as onions or potatoes or spices and were a kitchen staple like flour or sugar, and so they should be again. Kitchens of long ago were filled with their mouth-watering fragrance, as many old cookbooks testify. Use your imagination with nuts, just as your grandmother used hers.

Nuts can be made to disappear by adding them to foods after they have been ground, yet all the nutritive qualities are still there. For a different texture you may even combine chopped and ground nuts in the same dish, or use two different nuts.

Most of the nut recipes in this book can be used interchangeably. You can substitute Walnuts for Pecans, Filberts for Almonds or Peanuts. For economy's sake you can use less meat and more nuts. For flavor's sake you can use nuts toasted or plain, blanched or unblanched, chopped or whole. Almost all nuts have a definite affinity for bread. Use them throughout the year, not just at holiday time.

I will grant you that nuts once were easier to come by, often free for the gathering. This is no longer true. They now are quite high in price, as a quick look at the grocery shelf will tell you. But remember they still can be free for you — if you will plant your own. And, if everybody with a bit of land would plant just a few trees there would be nuts enough for all!

GENERAL NURSERIES

This is a partial list of firms selling nut trees. The inclusion of a firm is not a guarantee of reliability, and the absence does not imply disapproval.

Burgess Seed & Plant Co.,
Box 218, Galesburg, Michigan 49053
  Blizzard Belt Nut Trees — Burgess Hardy English Walnut, Filberts or Hazelnuts, Pecans, Hardy Almonds, Peanuts (Early Spanish)

Burpee Seeds, P.O. Box 6929,
Philadelphia, Pa. 19132
  Peanuts — (Jumbo Virginia and Early Spanish)

Earl May Seed & Nursery Co.
Shenandoah, Iowa 51601
  Carpathian Walnut, Hardy Pecan, Chinese Chestnut, Black Walnuts, Hazelnuts, Shellbark Hickory, Peanuts (Mammoth Jumbo)

Gurney Seed & Nursery Co.,
Yankton, S.D., 57078
  Carpathian Walnut, Hickory, Japanese Heart Nut, Black Walnut, Chinese Chestnut, Hall's Hardy Almond, Butternut, Hazelnut, Pecan, Turkish Filbert and Manchurian Walnut, Peanuts (Early Spanish)

Henry Field Seed & Nursery Co.
Shenandoah, Iowa 51602
  Chinese Chestnut, Butternut, Shellbark (Kingnut) Hickory, Carpathian Walnut, Hazelnut, Black Walnut, Hardy Pecans, Peanuts (Jumbo) (Early Spanish)

Inter-State Nurseries
Hamburg, Iowa 51640
  Carpathian Walnuts, Thomas Black Walnuts, Pecans, Chinese Chestnuts

Mellinger's
2310 West South Range Rd., North Lima, Ohio 44452
  Pinyon Pine

Geo. W. Park Seed Co., Inc.
Greenwood, S.C. 29646
    Park's Whopper Peanut (Avg. 2¾ in. long), Red Tennessee

Sierra Gold Nurseries
P.O. Box 815, Yuba City, California
    Carmelo Walnuts (large as small peaches), Almonds
    (Calico)

Spring Hill Nurseries
Tipp City, Iowa 45366
    Dwarf American Hazelnut, Hardy Pecan, Black Walnut,
    American Butternut, Hardy Almond, Chinese Chestnut,
    Carpathian Walnut, Peanuts (Jumbo)

Stark Bros.,
Louisiana, Mo. 63353
    Carpathian Walnut, Kwik-Krop Black Walnut, Chinese
    Chestnut, Butternut, American Hazelnut, Missouri Mam-
    moth Hickory Nut, Pecans (Grafted), Hardy Pecans

Stern's Nurseries
Geneva, N.Y. 14456
    Hazelnuts, Carpathian Walnuts, Chinese Chestnut, Hardy
    Northern Pecans

Stokes Seeds, Inc.
Box 548, Buffalo, N.Y. 14240
    Peanuts (Early Spanish)

R. H. Shumway
Rockford, Ill. 61101
    Halls Hardy Almond, Carpathian Walnut, Hardy Pecan,
    Thomas Black Walnut, Butternut, Chinese Chestnut, Fil-
    berts, Peanuts (Mammoth Jumbo) (Early Spanish)

Wolfe Nursery
Hwy 377 West
Stephenville, Texas 76401
    Pecans, Carpathian Walnut, Thomas Black Walnut

NUT TREE NURSERIES

Coble's Nut Nursery, Route 1, Aspers, Pennsylvania 17304

Earl Douglass, Red Creek, N.Y. 13143 — Hybrid Chestnut Seed

Green Country Nut Tree Nursery, Chas. G. Haines, R. 1, Cedarville, Ohio 45314

Green Haven Farm Nursery, R. 1, Perrinton, Michigan 48871

Louis Gerardi Nursery, Rt. 1, O'Fallon, Illinois 62269. Also has scionwood of all nut trees available. Place orders for scionwood before end of February.

Kelly Bros. Nurseries, Inc., 23 Maple Street, Dansville, N.Y. 14437

Miller Bros. Nursery, 5060 West Lake Road, Canandaigua, N.Y. 14424

Ozark Nurseries, Rt. 2, Tahlequah, Okla. 74464

Pataky Nursery, 610 Hickory Lane, Mansfield, Ohio 44905

Talbott Nursery, Rt. 3, Linton, Inc. 47441

Valley View Nursery, 748 S. Queen St., York, Pa. 17403

Zilke Bros. Nursery, Princess Anne, Md. 21853

NUT TREE INFORMATION

Northern Nut Growers Association
Att: Mr. Spencer B. Chase, Secretary-Treasurer
4518 Holston Hills Road
Knoxville, Tenn. 37914

Stronghold
4931 Upston Street, N.W.
Washington, D. C. 20016 This organization is interested in bringing back the American Chestnut and hope to eventually breed a blight-resistant type.

GENERAL INFORMATION

Power tools for woodworking:

Dremel Manufacturing Company
P.O. Box 518
Racine, Wisconsin 53401

Findings for making wooden jewelry:

Grieger's, Inc.
Dept. 19
1633 E. Walnut St.
Pasadena, Calif. 91109

Recipe booklet (Free — enclose stamp)

Oklahoma Peanut Commission
Box D
Madill, Oklahoma 73446

Nutcrackers:

The New Dynamic Nutcracker
L. H. Powell
8647 Wingate
Dallas, Texas 75209

Earl May Seed & Nursery Co.
Shenandoah, Iowa 51601

York Nut Sheller, Inc.
P.O. Box 928
San Angelo, Texas 76901

The New Weber Nut Cracker
W. O. Weber
201 Rose Marie Lane
Ft. Walton Beach, Florida 32548

U.S.D.A. and Standard Varieties

NOTE: While it is impossible to provide a complete list of nurserymen with Pecan trees and propagation wood, this list is furnished with the understanding that no discrimination intended and no guarantee of reliability is implied.
*These sources have propagation wood only.

Aldridge Nursery, Inc.
Route 1
Von Ormy, Texas 78073

Archer Pecan Nursery
P.O. Box 68
Rincon, New Mexico 87940

*Barnett Springs Ranch
c/o C. E. Tisdale
San Saba, Texas 76877

Bass Pecan Company
P.O. Box 42
Lumberton, Miss. 39455

Bright's Nursery
5246 South Plainsburg Road
Le Grand, Calif. 95333

Cockrell's Riverside Nursery
Route 1, Box 58
Goldthwaite, Texas 76844

Comanche Pecan Nursery
c/o J. E. Shaw
Comanche, Texas 76442

*David Fant
507 Spring Street
Weatherford, Texas 76086

Fitzgerald Nursery
Stephenville, Texas 76401

O. S. Gray Nursery
P. O. Box 550
Arlington, Texas 76010

Gro-Plant Industries
P. O. Box 160
Monticello, Florida 32344

H & H Wholesale Nursery
P.O. Box 1078
Las Cruces, N.M. 88001

*Johnny Harris
P. O. Box 191
Hamilton, Texas 76531

Irvington Nursery
Irvington, Alabama 36544

Linwood Nursery
3607 W. Linwood Ave.
Turlock, Calif. 95380

Chester Marrs Nursery
Route 1
Ranger, Texas 76470

Ozark Nurseries
Route 2
Tahlequah, Okla. 74464

U.S.D.A. and Standard Varieties (Continued)

Pair Nursery
Route 6
Dublin, Texas 76446

Wells Nursery
Box 146, Route 3
Lindale, Texas 75771

*Will Sidney Price
Box 86
Kerens, Texas 75144

Wolfe Nursery
Box 811
Stephenville, Texas 76401

Stahmann Farms Inc.
Box 500
Las Cruces, N.M. 88001

Womack's Nursery
Route 1
De Leon, Texas 76444

Texas Pecan Nursery
P. O. Box 306
Chandler, Texas 75758

SOURCES FOR NORTHERN VARIETIES

Earl Cully
R.R. 5
Jacksonville, Ill. 62650

Stark Bro's Nurseries
Louisiana, Mo. 63353

Louis Gerardi Nursery
R.R. 1
O'Fallon, Illinois 62269

John Talbott
Route 3
Linton, Indiana 47441

Greiner & Sons
Box 70
Mulvane, Kansas 67110

Indiana Nut Nursery
Route 3
Rockport, Indiana 47635

Ozark Nurseries
Route 2
Tahlequah, Okla. 74464

INDEX

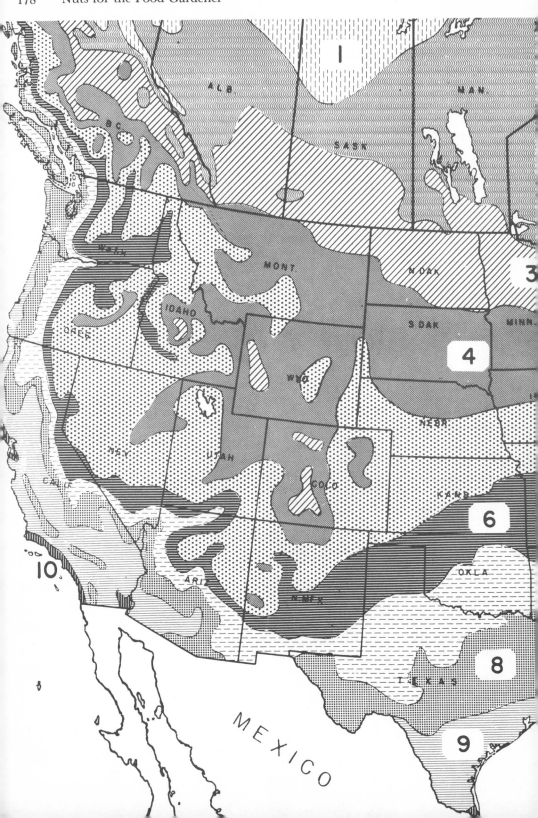

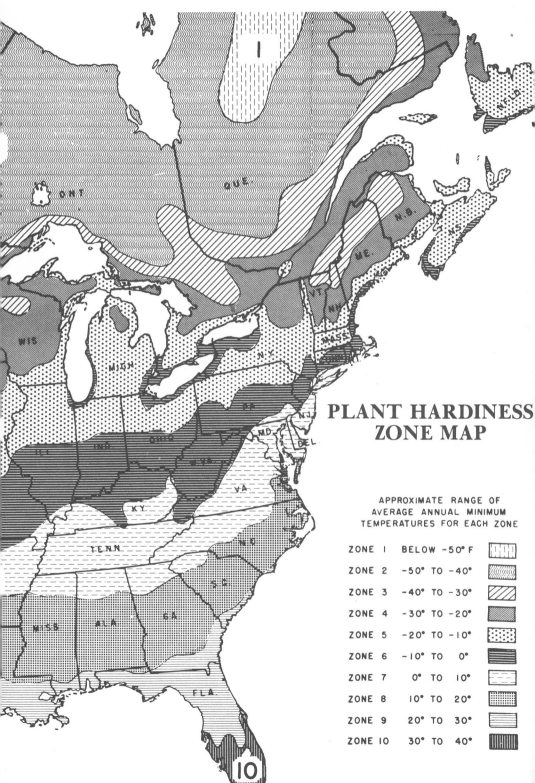

PLANT HARDINESS ZONE MAP

APPROXIMATE RANGE OF
AVERAGE ANNUAL MINIMUM
TEMPERATURES FOR EACH ZONE

ZONE 1	BELOW −50° F
ZONE 2	−50° TO −40°
ZONE 3	−40° TO −30°
ZONE 4	−30° TO −20°
ZONE 5	−20° TO −10°
ZONE 6	−10° TO 0°
ZONE 7	0° TO 10°
ZONE 8	10° TO 20°
ZONE 9	20° TO 30°
ZONE 10	30° TO 40°